MW01075343

How to Publish and Promote Online

HOW TO PUBLISH
AND PROMOTE ONLINE

M. J. ROSE AND
ANGELA ADAIR-HOY

St. Martin's Griffin
New York

An earlier version of this book was published as an e-book entitled *The Secrets of Our Success: How to Successfully Publish and Promote on the Web—With Over 500 Links.* First published in Deep South Publishing Company by Booklocker.com.

HOW TO PUBLISH AND PROMOTE ONLINE. Copyright © 2001 by M. J. Rose and Angela Adair-Hoy. All rights reserved. Printed in the United States of America. No part of this book may be used or reproduced in any manner whatsoever without written permission except in the case of brief quotations embodied in critical articles or reviews. For information, address St. Martin's Press, 175 Fifth Avenue, New York, NY 10010.

www.stmartins.com

BOOK DESIGN BY CASEY HAMPTON

ISBN 0-312-27191-3

First Edition: January 2001

10 9 8 7 6 5 4 3 2 1

CONTENTS

In this book we mention many companies, resources, and individuals that offer a variety of services, including Angela's own e-book publishing company, Booklocker.com. We even recommend a few. We have run into some wonderful people, Web sites, and companies and share them here.

We don't guarantee anyone's work mentioned in this book, however. We urge you to do your homework and check contracts, credentials, and references before doing business with anyone. On the Internet prices, companies, and services change at hyper speed.

In these pages are the opinions of expert authorities in many fields. The use of these opinions is no substitute for professional services to suit your specific personal needs. Always consult a competent professional for answers to your specific questions.

Please note: All chapters that don't list an individual author are the work of both M. J. Rose and Angela Adair-Hoy.

INTRODUCTION

M. J. Rose

We writers dream of seeing our names on the spine of a book on a bookstore shelf. Yet more and more that aspiration is becoming not only an impossible dream but an old-fashioned one. Publishers are looking for the big books, the bestsellers, the ones that market themselves on the author's name alone. And many of us can't meet that criterion.

Yet that isn't the bad news it used to be. Now there is an evolution going on. The Internet is making authors into publishers and readers into reviewers and all bets are off as to where this will wind up. One thing is for sure. You *can* sell books on the Internet without the help of a publisher. Or you can work with a small publisher and get big results.

Once upon a time, I was stuck on the idea that if I didn't have a big publisher's imprint on my book, I wouldn't be a real writer. For five years I suffered with that delusion. Self-publishing seemed the self-indulgent act of an egoist. Small presses didn't get noticed and weren't as savvy about marketing as I wanted them to be. Besides, I had a big dream: A bookstore window filled with stacks of my book. And only a big publisher had the ability and distribution to make that happen. But after five years I had to face facts. My dream wasn't coming true.

So I let go of the big dream and turned to a very, very tiny one: I wanted someone to read my book. Just one other person.

I built a Web site and offered my novel for sale. And soon that dream of one reader became ten readers. The harder I worked the bigger the reality became. Soon I had a hundred readers . . . and then a thousand.

And now, looking back, what strikes me as the most important secret I can share is that, when your dreams are huge, you don't know where to start to make them come true. But if you scale down your dream to make it fit in the palm of your hand, you can accomplish something. And then the dream will grow on its own.

Little did I think my little dream would eventually lead to a book contract with a big New York publisher.

Little did my coauthor, Angela, think hers would lead to the kind of success that has enabled her to buy her own publishing company.

We hope this book will help you make your dreams become real. And that once real, they grow and grow.

One thing we know, the World Wide Web is one place where dreams do come true.

Angela Adair-Hoy

I had a dream, too. I wanted to eat! My career began in the right place (a television studio), got sidetracked (accountant, human resources administrator, bonsai grower, mother of three), and now sits just about where I left off ten years ago, with my name on a television screen . . . except now they call it a computer monitor.

Less than two years ago I was unemployed for the first time in thirteen years. I was recently divorced, leaving me a single mother of three. I received no child support. My refrigerator was broken, and my pantry was so bare it echoed. But God works in mysterious ways, and my desperate situation turned out to be the catapult for my publishing career.

So, please, come into my office (bedroom), have a seat (on the bed), and let me tell you how I did it.

One day I was sitting in my living room, laptop perched in front of my eyeballs, checking e-mails from readers of *WritersWeekly,* my e-magazine for freelance writers. I realized I had just typed the answer to the same basic question for the tenth time in one afternoon.

Yes, I had received the same question, though worded differently, from ten different writers in one day. The question they all asked was how to make and sell e-books. My creative gears began to churn.

First, I realized that there was no source of information on e-books yet. Second, I knew everything about e-books. I was one of the first authors on the globe to convert a print book into an e-book. I was also the first publisher to convert a print, subscription-based magazine to an electronic-only, subscription-based publication. Finally, I had unknowingly written many of the rules of e-publishing as I went along.

I could help these people! I could use my knowledge and provide it in e-book format (of course).

I put my laptop on the floor and jumped up . . . really high. (I do that when I get excited.) I just *knew* I had a winning idea and I couldn't wait to get started! I heated up a quick dinner for my three children and told them that I would need to write, uninterrupted, that evening. They understood.

I sat down at four P.M. and wrote and wrote and wrote. I didn't stop to answer e-mail. I stopped once to go to the bathroom. I let the kids stay up late watching TV so I wouldn't have to take a break to bathe and tuck them in. (They didn't mind at all.) I did not use an outline. I did not stop and ponder every thought. I just typed until my fingers cramped, paused to crack my knuckles, and typed on and on.

At ten P.M., I was finished. And, I knew, deep down in my soul, that it was damned good. (I would save editing and formatting for the following day.) I turned off the computer and went to bed, but I could hardly sleep because of my excitement. I knew I had done something very good, something that would help others do what I had done . . . something that might even change the entire traditional publishing industry. I was never more proud of myself than I was at that moment.

The next morning I got the kids off to school and finished editing that day's issue of *WritersWeekly*. I went ahead and put a big, shameless ad in there for my new book, thinking that people would need to see the ad for an issue or two before they'd actually buy the book.

Wrong!

I clicked "send" and got up to do a load of dishes. Five minutes later, I was back to check for bounced messages. No bounces had come through . . . but thirteen e-mails marked "PRIORITY ORDER" were in my in-box. Thirteen? *Thirteen orders in five minutes?!* It was no mistake. In five minutes, with no printing costs, I had just made $116.35. Holy cow! I couldn't believe it then, and I still can't believe it. By the end of the day, I had processed more than $400 in orders. The following day, they kept coming. By day three, I had made more than $1,000 on my new e-book.

So, what's happening now? Well, as expected, many copycats came out of the woodwork, especially after I told everyone who would listen about my book's instant success. However, mine is already revised to address new technologies (such as security issues and e-book pirating), and the others, while they may fool some, can't teach originality and the launching of new ideas, since they copied me.

I know that sharing my story will inspire writers to do what I have done. If I can do it, anyone can.

Finally . . . my secret. I have never taken a formal writing course and I don't intend to. I write the way I talk. This, I believe, is what keeps my readers coming back for more. They can hear my voice through my words and they feel as though they know me, my personality, my life . . . and that I understand them as well. I've been there. Writers are starving artists. I've been forced to skip a few meals when assignments were slow and money was absent. But, far above that, I understand the desire to write and the desire to make a living doing what you love.

Whatever you can do,
Or dream you can do,
Begin it.
Boldness has genius, power and magic in it.
Begin it now.

—GOETHE

Part One

EVERYTHING YOU NEED TO KNOW ABOUT PUBLISHING ON- AND OFFLINE

SO YOU'VE WRITTEN A BOOK . . . WHAT'S NEXT?

M. J. Rose

So you've written a book and haven't been able to get one of the top ten big publishing houses to publish it.

That puts you in good company. More writers are rejected by the big houses than are accepted. But the Internet has given writers opportunities that never existed before. Every day, books are discovered through the new alternative publishing channels.

The most difficult challenge for any author today is *not* getting published. It's deciding what publishing option to choose and then figuring out how to get noticed.

E-publishing is flourishing. Estimates are that by the end of this year over seventy thousand previously unpublished books and shorter works will be available online or through print-on-demand (POD). Some industry analysts suggest the number will be closer to half a million.

The real challenge for a writer is finding readers. It takes two things: A good book and a good marketing plan.

As we try to help you figure out how to accomplish those goals we are going to be using some words and phrases that apply more to advertising than to publishing. That's because getting a book in front of the public is a promotional tour de force, one to which you need to apply all the same creativity and determination that you applied to writing your magnum opus in the first place.

And this is true whether you have a big publisher helping you or a small publisher helping you or you are doing it alone because, except for the top one hundred or so bestselling authors, we all do some or most of our own promotion.

The trick to marketing your title is thinking outside the box. If you come up with an idea that no one has tried before, that's the first place to start.

When we first started publishing our e-books, no one was even using the word e-book. We were calling our efforts electronic downloads. Now we have e-books and a myriad of devices on which to read them. There are several formats that these books are available in and even more Web sites on which to list your book for sale.

There are hundreds of electronic publishers (e-publishers) and print-on-demand (POD) publishers who only work in the new electronic formats. Even more writer and reader Web sites offer knowledge, reviews, and promotional opportunities for enterprising authors. There is even an e-book club, *www.ebooksonthe.net,* with a monthly featured selection, similar to the traditional book clubs.

Readers have become critics (thanks to sites like Amazon.com, which pioneered reader reviews), authors are becoming publishers, and the future never looked rosier for every writer out there. So where do you start?

IN THE BEGINNING . . .

M. J. Rose

It used to be that if a book could not find a home at a publishing company, it probably wasn't very good. Today that is simply not true.

The advent of the superstore bookstore, the decline of the independent bookstore, the mergers of so many publishing houses, and the megadeals top authors get have all drastically lowered the number of new authors published each year.

There are far too many good manuscripts being passed over these days. Some because they are good but not good enough. Some because they don't fit a genre. Some because they appeal to too small an audience.

Most big publishers want books that can sell at least 25,000 copies.

But if you publish your own book or work with an electronic publisher, you can make a profit on only 3,000 copies, if you do it right.

So how do you know if your book is worth publishing on the Internet? Well, not because your best friend loves it.

You should consider going the traditional route first. Try to get an agent and a deal with a respected publishing house that has national distribution in bookstores both on- and offline. Those big houses do have serious marketing money. They do have good editors and publicity departments. And they do give advances.

But if you get rejected, don't crawl into a corner and sulk. Ask the agent to let you see the rejection letters. Read between the lines. Understand that editors and marketing departments are looking for reasons *not* to buy a book. When they can't find any, that's the book they take. No publishing company has the funds to take chances on maybes anymore.

If you can't get an agent, there is usually a good reason. So before you self-publish a book that even an agent won't take, look around for some writing courses and workshops. There are some wonderful ones cropping up on the Internet. Join them! Put your ego on hold and listen hard to what other writers say about your work.

PROFESSIONAL EDITING IS A MUST

Whether you plan to self-publish your book or work with an e-publishing house, you need to invest in your work. Almost none of the online publishing companies edit books to the extent that every book needs to be edited.

Once you're happy with your book, you should hire a freelance book doctor or editor to read the manuscript, make corrections, and give you a professional opinion. This step is critical. There will be literally hundreds of thousands of books published on the Internet every year, and your book is competing with every single one of them. You want to put your best effort out there because you only get one chance with a reader.

No matter how terrific a writer you are, it's almost impossible to edit your own work and see what's missing. That's why, even if you have to get a freelance job to raise the money, you need to hire a professional editor.

Be careful in choosing one; check out the editor's reputation with several people. Get references. Protect yourself from people who are just trying to get your money and don't have credentials.

A great way to get those recommendations is to talk to other writers who have used editors. But what if you don't know other writers? You can meet thousands who can help you with the names of editors and proofreaders (as well as commiserate, encourage, give you the scoop on different e-publishers, and a variety of other subjects) on the Web by joining some of the writing discussion lists that you can find online and in this book.

These groups of like-minded people are called listservs. For every interest you have you can find one of these lists. There are millions of them online. When you join a listserv the proper etiquette is to lurk (read but do not participate) for a week or so and get the tone of the discussion and the formality or informality of that particular group. Once you feel comfortable, jump on in. Introduce yourself and ask for help. We've found these groups to be friendly, supportive, and full of information.

We can't emphasize enough the need to have your book edited. Your book must be copyedited and proofread and look just as professional as any other book out there. You are competing with Stephen King and Nora Roberts whether you like it or not.

You don't want to lose your credibility with a reader when he or she opens your novel and finds typos and grammatical errors in the first paragraph. Believe me, you won't get a second chance with that reader.

One thing about the Internet is the speed with which information is passed around the globe. If one reader finds errors in your book, he or she can literally let thousands and even millions of people online know about it. One bad book review at a high-traffic Web site can make or break an author. Your book must be perfect before you sell the very first copy.

When your book is as perfect as it can be, it's time to get it out there in the hands of buyers!

WHAT IS AN E-BOOK?

Angela Adair-Hoy

An e-book is a book delivered in electronic format, as an electronic document, which must be accessed using a computer. Some e-books are delivered as electronic downloads to a buyer's computer, and some are sent via electronic mail (e-mail), while others are sent via regular mail on a CD-ROM or computer disk to the buyer. Most readers print the e-books they buy to read later, while some are content to read their e-books on their desktop or laptop computers, or handheld devices.

An e-book is really no different from a nicely formatted word processing document, so don't let the term "electronic" frighten you. Even a beginner computer user can turn a text manuscript into a beautiful e-book.

Most e-books resemble print books in formatting. They feature attractive cover art (computer graphics), a table of contents, page numbers, and other print book qualities. These e-books are very easy to read on computers and also to print. Some e-books are created using special computer programs that make it appear as though the reader's computer is making pages turn. Still other e-books are created with links, buttons in the document that, when clicked with the reader's mouse, take the reader to another chapter instantly, or even to a Web site if their computer is online while they're reading the e-book. Finally, some e-books have sounds and moving pictures. I call those interactive e-books.

As in print publishing, the price range for e-books is broad. Readers can purchase small e-booklets of around fifty pages or less for as little as two dollars. Some e-books are professional reference books with specific audience demographics. These e-books, like their print reference counterparts, can cost upward of a hundred dollars or more. The average consumer non-fiction e-book costs around ten to twenty dollars, while consumer fiction usually costs less.

SELL YOUR TITLE IN BOTH E-BOOK AND PRINT FORMATS

There are only two distribution formats to consider: print and electronic. But there are a myriad of options under each of these.

PRINT

You can pay a printer to print your book, you can hire a vanity publisher to do it, or you can go through a print-on-demand (POD) firm. We discuss all of these options in this section.

ELECTRONIC

You can design your own e-book or pay a firm to design it for you. You can publish your own e-book and sell it through your Web site, via e-mail, or by mail on CD-ROM. Or you can list your book with an e-publisher and trade part of your book's profits for their services. These options, too, are discussed in detail in this section.

We recommend publishing your book as an e-book and paying for a short print run or printing through POD. There are several reasons we suggest publishing in both formats.

The advantages of e-books are the low production cost and the instant gratification for your customers who want to start reading your book within seconds.

The advantage of having a print book available as well is that not everyone wants to read a novel on a reading device. Most people still want to curl up in bed with a good book, and not everyone owns a handheld reader or a laptop computer, enabling them to read in bed. Another reason is that not everyone wants to print out a three-hundred-page book on their own printer. Some review sources will not yet review e-books or e-galleys. To get your books reviewed, you usually need printed copies, although *Publishers Weekly* and *ForeWord Magazine* do review e-books.

HOW TO CREATE AN E-BOOK

Angela Adair-Hoy

First and foremost, if you want to publish and promote e-books online, you must have access to a computer that has a word processing program on it. You will also need Internet access for many of the resources recommended in this book.

ELECTRONIC TEXT

Your book must be in some sort of electronic format. It can be a text-only document, or formatted using a word processor. If your book is only in print and you do not have an electronic version of the text, you will either need to retype the entire book yourself or hire someone to do it for you. One alternative is to hire a local college student to help.

I do not recommend scanning your manuscript or out-of-print book with a scanner. A scanner makes a graphic file by taking a picture of the document being scanned, much like a copy machine. Graphic files are large, and scanned books can grow to enormous byte proportions. One romance novelist scanned her existing romance novels, a time-consuming task similar to flipping pages in a book and making photocopies of every single page. While the books were only around two hundred pages apiece, each one ended up as a document of more than twenty megs because every page was converted to a graphic file. An e-book this large is huge for readers' computers, and the vast majority of computers will choke on a file of this size, especially if the buyer is trying to download the file. So e-books should be in electronic text to begin with.

There are programs that can pull text from graphic files, but affordable ones are prone to errors and the author will end up retyping most of the text anyway.

TEXT TO ATTRACTIVE TEXT

The next step is to turn your existing plain text document into an attractive e-book, complete with styled chapter headings, page numbers, a table of contents, and more. How do you do that? Different word processing programs have different specific instructions but we can give you a head start.

Booklocker.com, the e-publishing company that I co-own, has a sample e-book in Microsoft Word format that anyone can download. Microsoft Word is the most popular word processing program in use today. If you have any up-to-date word processing program, it will probably be able to open and recognize this document with ease.

The sample e-book includes a title page, table of contents, footers (the book title appears at the bottom of each page), page numbers, and basic instructions for making your e-book look like a real book when viewed on a computer screen. You can even copy and paste your own graphics into the sample e-book.

Hundreds of writers download this sample e-book every day, and few have difficulty understanding it. It has simple instructions such as "type your book's title here" and "insert information about the author here."

You can download the sample e-book at *www.booklocker.com/sampleebook.zip*. If your word processing program isn't compatible with Microsoft Word, you can download the PDF version to see the style used at *www.booklocker.com/samplepdfebook.zip*. (For more on PDF documents, see the end of this chapter.)

Basic E-Book Formatting

E-book formatting can be quite flexible and creative, and include a variety of fonts, colors, pictures, and even links to Web sites.

For starters, the paragraphs in your book should be no more than four to six sentences. Don't ramble. If a paragraph is noticeably long, cut it in half. Readers get lost in long paragraphs, especially if they're reading your book on their monitor. Keep it short, simple, and easy to read.

Even more important than the title, is a cover image. Even for e-books, you should have cover art! Cover art is what catches a reader's eyes and makes them click. If you don't know how to design an electronic book cover, find a friend who does or hire a graphic artist to design one for you.

RECOMMENDED E-BOOK CONTENTS

Title Page

If you don't have cover art, you can type the title of your book using a very large font. You can even change the color of the type to your liking. Then you should access the borders function of your word processing program and draw a border around the entire page, making the cover look like a book cover.

Copyright Page

Your copyright page specifies that your book is, indeed, copyrighted. It presents specific instructions to readers about what they may *not* do with your e-book. The copyright page should include standard copyright terms (found in printed books), but should also address electronic transmission. The following statement appears in all of my e-books:

> Published by Angela Adair-Hoy, My Address, City, State, Zip Code. E-mail aadair@writersweekly.com © year Angela Adair-Hoy. All rights reserved. No part of this publication may be reproduced, stored in a retrieval system, or transmitted in any form or by any means, electronic, mechanical, recording or otherwise, without the prior written permission of the author.

Dedication Page (optional)

Authors dedicate their book to a person or persons on the dedication page.

Table of Contents

Used primarily for nonfiction, a table of contents lists the chapter numbers and titles and gives their page numbers.

About the Author

In my e-books, I insert a picture of myself along with a short bio. Having an electronic picture of yourself on your e-book really lends a personal touch. If you download the sample e-book at Booklocker.com, you'll see how this is done.

Introduction

This short section gives the reader a jump-start into the book, and often serves the same purpose as the "flap copy" found on printed book jackets. If you skipped the introductions in this book, go back and read them to see how we motivated the reader to keep on reading! The introduction is a teaser. Along with a book's cover, this is the section that buyers read in bookstores to determine if they will buy the book or not. Many authors offer the introductions to their e-books free online as a marketing tool when promoting their books online. Many also post the introduction on e-publishers' Web sites as a long description of their book.

Chapters

For e-books, I recommend a sixteen-point font, in bold, for chapter headings, and a fourteen-point font size, not bold, for the actual book text. These sizes do not waste space and are easy to read on a computer screen.

Glossary (primarily for nonfiction)

If you have used specific terms that readers may need to look up, create a glossary at the end of your e-book, just as if you were creating a printed book. If you have the technical skills, you can make your glossary link back to the contents of your book so that readers will be able to click to find every instance where each term was used.

SOFTWARE

HTML

While most e-books are initially created using a word processing program, some writers are computer savvy enough to go one or two steps further. Some e-books are created using HTML (hypertext markup language). This is the computer code used to create most Web pages. It isn't too difficult to learn, but it is also not at all mandatory in order to create e-books. There are computer programs that will convert your word processing document into HTML automatically. Most handheld e-book readers require e-books to be in HTML.

PDF

I began publishing e-books in 1997, before anyone knew what an e-book was . . . myself included. One problem I encountered when distributing my e-books was incompatibility between my personal computer (PC) word processing documents and Macintosh (Mac) word processing programs. Lots of people use Macs, and I wanted to be able to sell my e-books to everyone, but I wanted to offer only one format. I found it!

PDF (portable document format) files are created using Adobe Acrobat. This common type of electronic format allows readers with any type of computer (Mac or PC) to read and print a document using Adobe Acrobat Reader, which anyone (including your customers) can download free at *www.adobe.com*. The software does not allow readers to manipulate the PDF document in any way, so you don't have to worry about someone cutting and pasting your text into their own document and using it as their own.

As a lone publisher starting out, you might not be able to afford Adobe Acrobat, the software required to create and distribute PDF documents. However, anyone can convert five documents to PDF for free at the Adobe Web site here: *createpdf.adobe.com*. If you don't want to do it yourself, you can order a $15 quick conversion from my *WritersWeekly* Web site *www.writersweekly.com/bookediting.htm*.

Adobe Acrobat is around $180 at Buy.com (*www.buy.com*). You'll find it for $249 at most places, including the large office supply chains. Some colleges offer the software at a discount to students for only around $99.

It is also possible to publish and distribute your e-book as a text-only document. Remember, however, that the appearance of your book influences how its quality is perceived, regardless of your content. Even if you are a novice, we highly suggest you begin by distributing your book as a PDF document.

SECURITY

If you're worried about someone taking your book, reformatting it, and reselling it, don't. You're going to copyright your work (more on that later), and there are ways to stop copyright infringement. If I did not publish electronically for fear of e-book pirating, I'd already be out of business.

Finally, technology will soon enable encryption on every e-book. Self-publishers will be able to prevent their e-books being e-mailed, copied, and uploaded. Adobe recently released this type of software, but is asking $5,000 for it. Uh, no thanks. We'll wait for a cheaper version.

ALL E-DONE!

Once you've formatted your e-book and it's ready for delivery, e-mail it to yourself as an attachment (if you don't know how to do this, search for the word "attach" in the help section of your mail program). This is to make sure that the formatting isn't being distorted upon delivery to your readers. E-mail, send, receive, open, and save the document again under a different name. Check all formatting thoroughly to make sure it came through the phone line intact. If you have your own Web site, upload your e-book and then download it to see how it survives the trip.

DESIGNING YOUR BOOK AND ITS COVER

C. Mayapriya Long

The cliché may say you shouldn't, but the fact is that many people, at least at first, do judge a book by its cover. Whether we are browsing a traditional bookstore or an Internet one, our eye stops when it is attracted by pleasing design, by type that expresses the subject well, or by a pertinent or interesting photo.

If a book is going to be reviewed by the media, stocked by bookstores, and opened by your audience, it has to give a favorable first impression. It has to say, in essence, "I am interesting, authoritative, and professionally presented. You will not be disappointed if you spend your hard-earned money on me." Even if the content is superior, no one will ever know how good the content is if the cover fails to atttract the reader. And if the interior design makes the flow of the information difficult to follow and understand, the book may be set aside before much of it has been read.

E-books are no different. The trend is rapidly moving toward making the e-book reading experience more closely resemble reading a print book. E-book audiences will want your book to have the same pleasant page layout as print books. And they already want to see cover art that convinces them they are buying a book of substance.

DO YOU NEED A BOOK DESIGNER?

For book interiors of a print-on-demand or conventionally printed book, you need a designer if you are not familiar with paging software such as

PageMaker, Quark XPress, Framemaker, InDesign, or others. Word processing software is great for use as you write your manuscript but it is not made for producing book pages. Except in the hands of an extremely skilled practitioner, word processing software falls short of producing really first-class pages. So unless you fall into the category above, hire a professional. If you are planning to produce your e-book in PDF format, it will be easy for your designer to make PDF files from the same files you will use for a print-on-demand book.

For the text of e-books, you will most likely be using the same word processing files that make up your manuscript. For facilitating the conversion to HTML format, you want to make sure not to use smart quotes or em dashes. Talk to your e-book publisher, or if you are your own e-book publisher, get ideas from other publisher's sites about preparing manuscripts for them.

Book covers should always be produced by a design professional. If you are an artist, you may still want to hire a designer and supply her/him with your drawing or painting.

Book cover design is a particular specialty in graphic design. And it is not being overly critical to say that a good graphic designer who has never produced book covers is a bad choice. Hire someone whose specialty is books. There are many to choose from.

IS THERE A SECRET TO FINDING A GOOD DESIGNER?

When talking with a prospective designer for your book or cover, ask to see samples of the designer's work. Many have Web pages for viewing their work, but feel free to ask for actual printed covers or book interior samples to look over. Pick a designer who has a solid reputation and substantial track record and whose work you like. Ask for and call the references they give. You may pay slightly less for a person who is just starting their design business, but they may cost you more in the long run because of their lack of experience.

Since you will likely be producing an e-book, a print version (either print-on-demand or conventionally printed), and perhaps a CD-ROM version, you will want to know if your designer has experience in all three. While e-book cover design is very similar to conventional cover design, there are some differences. For instance, if your e-book will be read on a Rocket eBook, it will be in grayscale. The cover should translate nicely for this type of viewing. Also, e-book covers are generally viewed very small. Your cover design has to be attractive and, at least the title (if not the subtitle), should be legible at a small size. Not every word on the cover need be legible in the small e-book version since the description is usually right next to it on the Web site.

Your print or e-book has 3–4 seconds to attract a book buyer's attention, so a good designer is someone who can produce a cover that fits in with the other books in your genre, but also stands out from them.

Make sure your designer knows printing. Lots can go wrong and money can be wasted by amateurs. A good book designer will know what the industry standards are, how to get the best results from a printer, and will be able to send your electronic files to your printer or e-book publisher so that there will be no problems or headaches for you—and no unhappy surprises when you see your finished books.

WHAT'S THE SECRET TO GETTING THE COVER DESIGN YOU WANT?

- Your designer will want to please you and will also have her/his own ideas of how best to "show" your book. If you make a list of books with covers you like, this will help your designer visualize a design in a style you will find pleasing. If you have certain things you don't like, tell the designer those as well.

- Write up a one-page synopsis of your book and supply a table of contents. Few designers have time to read a manuscript before they design a cover. A good designer will be too busy working with clients to do that much reading!

- Supply every piece of text that will appear on the front, spine, and back cover. Indicate which text is the most important and hence should be made most prominent. If you want your company's logo to appear, you will need to supply a graphic file of that logo (or hire the designer to create that as well). You will need to give the designer your ISBN number and price so that they can supply a bar code for the back of the book. You will need to research shelving categories for the book (you can ask for your designer's advice on this also).

- Tell the designer who the audience is for the book. Some books cross over into more than one genre. Which is your biggest audience?

- Will the book be both an e-book and a print book? An e-book cover needs very clear, simple typography since it will be viewed primarily at a reduced size. If you are producing both, I would not recommend sacrificing the print cover design just because it will also be an e-book—but the fact that the book will be viewed in a very small version on sites such as Amazon.com and Barnes&Noble.com should be kept in mind.

- Will the print version be a paperback or hardcover book, or both? What is the trim size? Standard sizes most often used are 5½ x 8¼, 6⅛ x 9¼, and 8½ x 11 inches.
- How many colors can the designer use for the print version? Many think that a two- or three-color cover is much less expensive to print than a 4-color one. However, the difference is not as great as one might think, and for POD books, there is no difference in cost. Since a 4-color cover gives your designer more to work with, it increases the likelihood of your getting a more interesting and eye-catching cover.
- Do you have any photos or art you can supply for the cover? Do you want the designer to procure art? (You will have to pay for it but there are many royalty-free art sites where use of an image can be purchased for a reasonable fee.) Be up-front with your designer about your budget so they can plan a design that will fit within it.
- Do you have a preference for the typography? Do you like plain and simple or decorative type? E-book files that will be read in HTML don't have many fonts to choose from, but print books and PDF can use a variety.
- Is there a subtitle? Should it be emphasized?

Your designer will have other questions, but if you give them the information above, it should help them produce a cover you will like and, most important, will help you sell books. Good "packaging" is one of the secrets to selling more books both on and off the Internet. An attractive, professional-looking design gives reviewers confidence that the book inside is worth their valuable time, and will convince readers online and off that the product is worth the price to download.

Experienced publishers will tell you: Good book design is not an option to be placed at the bottom of the budget, to be had if money permits. It is a necessity. Remember, it is the visual poster for your words and usually the introduction to them as well.

C. Mayapriya Long is the owner of Bookwrights Book Design Studio and Bookwrights Press (*www.bookwrights.com*).

GOING FROM ELECTRONIC TO PRINT . . . AND VICE VERSA

Angela Adair-Hoy

Do some authors publish e-books and then start printing them all by themselves? Sure they do!

E-BOOK TO PRINT

If you are using a professional printer, they will have specific instructions for your book's submission. However, if you are going to attempt to print your own books or booklets and have them copied at your local copy shop, the steps are quite simple.

Formatting Books

- Change the font size of your book's body text to twelve points.
- Change the font size of your chapter titles to fourteen points.
- If your book will be black-and-white text only, change all font colors to black.
- Fonts with shadows and other odd characters should be changed to "regular."
- Buy ClickBook (from *www.bluesquirrel.com*). This program takes 8½-by 11-inch formatted documents and compresses them, turns them sideways, and enables you to print a book on your printer, in page order, front and back. I can't praise this program enough. I've even heard from some readers who have bought ClickBook just to be able to print and "bind" e-books they have purchased online.

Electronic Cover Art to Print Cover Art

Does your e-book's existing cover print well on paper? I almost always have to alter mine to make them cosmetically appealing in print. Print the cover, then run it through a copier, because this is what the copy shop will do. Then examine the quality to decide what you must do to make it a clean, printable cover.

Make sure your cover art will print nicely on whatever paper stock you choose. I recommend heavy paper, or even card stock, with at least a hint of color. Plain white, off-white, and gray are terribly bland. My recent choice is white stock with a hint of green marble. Pick a color that complements your topic and will appeal to your audience. For example, don't try to sell pink books to a male audience.

If you are interested in learning more about professional printers and in obtaining quotes from more than one hundred companies, don't miss the Aeonix Publishing Group Web site at *www.aeonix.com*.

PRINT BOOKS TO E-BOOKS

If you already publish in print, you should definitely go electronic, too, provided your print publisher doesn't hold your electronic rights. I took this road with my magazine and my first book. Sales soared and costs plummeted.

My book, *How to Be a Syndicated Newspaper Columnist* (*www.writersweekly. com/index-synd.htm*), began as a printed book. I only needed to convert the MSWord file to a readable online format and . . . voilà! I had published my first e-book.

Rights

Perhaps the rights to your print book belong to your publisher? Perhaps not? If your book is out of print, rights may have already reverted back to you. Go dig up your old contract and take a look.

If you do not hold electronic rights to your book, write a letter to your publisher explaining that you want to self-publish your book as an e-book now. Ask for a letter assigning electronic rights back to you. Publishers are much more aware of the popularity of the e-book industry than they were even a few months ago, so in some cases you will not be able to obtain your electronic rights. But, perhaps your publisher will oblige. If they don't, write another letter offering to pay *them* royalties on all sales if they allow you to self-publish and sell your e-book. It can't hurt to ask.

BECOMING A PUBLISHER . . .
ALL BY YOURSELF

Angela Adair-Hoy

If you're going to self-publish in print and electronically and do everything yourself, the effort is much greater, but so are the rewards. You'll be doing all the work, but you'll also be retaining 100 percent of your profits!

THE BUSINESS SIDE

So you want to open your own publishing business. Congratulations, you're now a true entrepreneur! Now, get ready for all the headaches that come with owning your own business.

The easiest way to start a small home-based business is to create a sole proprietorship. You can do this with a simple DBA (doing business as) certificate, which is quite inexpensive and sets the stage for opening your business bank account.

To obtain a DBA or to register your business with your local municipality, a quick phone call to your local county courthouse should get you started in the right direction. Different cities and counties have different requirements. Once you obtain your business certificate (or license) you can open a business bank account. Asking customers to make checks payable to a business rather than your name creates a much more professional impression.

Until I incorporated, I claimed my business income on Schedule C of my individual federal tax return (form 1040). It was quite simple. However, keeping track of all the receipts was a major headache. I countered my disorganization by hanging a big yellow envelope on the wall by my desk. In it, I put every little business expense receipt that inevitably ended up on my desk or in my computer bag (under the car seat, in the kids' toy box . . .).

If you choose to incorporate, you'll be at less personal risk should someone sue you, but the paperwork will be so much more! Consult your CPA or tax advisor to determine which choice is best for you.

START SMALL!

Do you need a business phone line? No. I think they're a waste of money when you're small. Just answer the phone using your name rather than your business name. I answer our phone, "Angela Hoy." Answering the phone this way sounds professional but doesn't confuse friends and neighbors.

Do you need a fancy fax machine? Heck no! Take advantage of the free online fax service offered by Efax.com (*www.efax.com*). Efax.com allows you to send and receive faxes online, and even gives you your own fax number.

ISBNs

If you are going to self-publish, you should have an International Standard Book Number (ISBN). If you look on the back cover of this book, you'll see a bar code with the ISBN on it. Libraries and bookstores can find you, as well as your book's price, a description, and ordering information, by using your book's ISBN.

You need to obtain an ISBN if you want to place your book at the big online booksellers. Another point to remember is that you need a different ISBN for each edition of your book: one for the paperback edition, one for the hardcover (if applicable), one for the e-book, and so on.

R. R. Bowker is the U.S. ISBN agency responsible for the assignment of ISBN Publisher Prefixes to publishers with a residence or office in the United States who are publishing their titles within the United States. Bowker's Web site (*www.bowker.com*) provides links to registry agencies outside of the United States as well.

Publishers enter the site and begin filling out a series of forms that register their publishing company and all the current products they have for sale. Then, they wait ten days for their Publisher Prefix. You have the option of paying an additional $50 to expedite your application, which will bring your ISBN Publisher Prefix within three days instead of ten.

Have your credit card handy and order your ISBN Publisher Prefix here: *www.bowker.com/standards/home/isbn*. (You can also find their contact information online if you prefer to pay by check.)

Getting an ISBN is a relatively simple process, but the cost is steep for the independent self-publisher at $205 for a block of ten ISBNs.

Don Riseborough, Senior Managing Editor, U.S. ISBN Agency, notes that "the $205 is a flat fee charged for processing each publisher application for an ISBN Publisher Prefix; it is *not* per ISBN. There is no other fee involved. A publisher is assured a minimum block of ten numbers."

What does this mean? Once you receive your Publisher Prefix, you can enter Bowker's Web site and add your books (and e-books) as they become available, as well as make updates to your existing products. Your products are then published in Bowker's periodicals such as *Books in Print*. You don't have to pay $205 for every new product you publish. You do, however, have to pay more later if you need more ISBNs than you receive from the initial block you purchased.

COPYRIGHTS

Once you write "Copyright © YEAR Your Name" on a document, it is copyrighted. However, should you ever need to prosecute someone else for infringing on your copyright, you need to have it registered. And, you need to register your copyright before someone else steals your material and copyrights it as their own. Copyrighting is easy and the cost is quite affordable. Get online and surf here: *www.loc.gov/copyright/forms*.

Print the forms, fill them out, follow the submission instructions, and get it over with. It's rather painless and only costs $30. You can save money by submitting multiple documents together for the same $30.

Copyright Infringement Abounds!
Anytime you publish a book, an e-mag, an article, or anything else online, there are unscrupulous authors and publishers waiting in the shadows to steal your work. Whether they are after your idea or your entire manuscript, if they find you're doing a better job than they are, they just might steal your copyrighted material and claim it as their own.

I can't even count how many times I have found my copyrighted material on other Web sites and in other e-mags. As a writer rallying for protecting copyrights, I was initially astounded at the gall of the first offender. Within hours, I managed to have her entire Web site shut down. I only needed to provide her Internet service provider (ISP) with a copy of my most recent issue and printed pages from her Web site that included my material. (I subsequently issued a press release titled, "How to Lose Your Web site with the Click of a Button," which generated a considerable amount of publicity.)

The following month, I found my list of markets (not similar markets, mind you, but my list, word-for-word) being *sold* in another electronic publication. I did not shut that site down, but instead gave them twenty-four hours to remove the offending material. I had some very harsh words with that publisher. He argued that contact information can't be copyrighted. I argued back that I had personally interviewed each editor to obtain their current needs and that he had committed copyright infringement of much more than simple contact information. He removed the material promptly and then offered to buy it from me on a continuing basis. I said no way. I don't do business with thieves, even ones who want to pay.

A print publication (published by someone I know) reprinted my list of markets without asking and without giving credit. She was extremely apologetic and provided an apology on the cover of her next issue. That generated many new subscribers for my e-mag, so that one didn't infuriate me as much as the others.

You, too, might find copyright violators. Register your copyrights now so you can protect your work if and when you need to.

How to Find Copyright Violators

There's a cool new site (*www.plagiarism.org*) designed for professors needing information on plagiarized papers. You can submit your manuscript to them with a simple upload and your first upload is free.

Plagiarism.org will respond in three to five days by e-mail with a list of Web pages that contain one or more exact phrases from the item you submit. While this won't work for information that does not appear on a Web page, it might catch marketing materials that use your words to promote your stolen material. Give it a try! You might be very surprised by what you find.

Our favorite publishing law Web site is *www.ivanhoffman.com*. It provides information on writing and publishing law, Web design contracts and law, copyrights, trademarks, Internet law, Web site audits, recording and music law, and much more.

When You Find a Copyright Violator

If you find your copyrighted material on another Web site, or anywhere else for that matter, take action quickly. Your first step is to contact the person who has stolen your material. A quick note telling them they are using your copyrighted material and an order to cease and desist will probably do the trick. However, sometimes this isn't enough.

If the violator has your material published on their Web site, you need to find out who owns the server their Web site is located on. You can do this by surfing to *www.register.com*. Type in the Web site's URL (for example, *www.writersweekly.com*). A screen will pop up, allowing you to click to view contact information of the site's owner. You can view their mailing address, phone numbers, e-mail addresses, and even the contact information for the firm hosting that site on their server.

If the offending Web site is a branch of a larger Internet Service Provider (ISP), you can usually simply type in the primary URL (domain name) to acquire contact information for the hosting service. For example, if the offending Web site is *members.tripod.com/copyrightviolator.html,* you can surf to *www.tripod.com* and find contact information for that hosting company.

Below is an example of a letter I sent to a hosting firm after finding my material on another Web site. I had previously contacted the ISP by phone and they requested documentation on the incident by e-mail. After sending this e-mail, the violator's site was taken off the Internet within one hour.

DATE

ATTN: [NAME OF INTERNET SERVICE PROVIDER]

CC: [NAME OF COPYRIGHT VIOLATOR]

PLEASE SEE BELOW PROOF THAT THE SITE OWNER IN QUESTION KNOWS THAT MY COPYRIGHTED MATERIAL APPEARS ON THEIR SITE AND HAS ALSO PROMISED TO FIX THE PROBLEM. HOWEVER, IT HAS BEEN MORE THAN A MONTH SINCE THIS CONFESSION WAS RECEIVED. THE MATERIAL APPEARING ON YOUR SERVER IS BLATANT COPYRIGHT INFRINGEMENT AND IS ILLEGAL. I DEMAND THE PAGE BE REMOVED FROM YOUR SERVER AT ONCE. BE AWARE THAT YOUR FIRM IS

NOW ALSO LEGALLY LIABLE FOR THIS MATTER AS YOU NOW KNOW ILLEGAL MA-
TERIAL EXISTS ON YOUR SERVER.

I EXPECT THIS MATTER TO BE RESOLVED WITHIN TWENTY-FOUR HOURS OR I
WILL NOT HESITATE TO TAKE QUICK ACTION. I AM AN ADVOCATE FOR WRITERS
AND THEIR RIGHTS, AND WE DO *NOT* TAKE COPYRIGHT INFRINGEMENT LIGHTLY.

ANGELA ADAIR-HOY
WRITERSWEEKLY.COM

CC: [MY LAWYER'S NAME]

9

FULFILLMENT AND DISTRIBUTION

Angela Adair-Hoy

So you've got your book edited, formatted, and ready to go. Now how do you set up a system for handling orders?

MERCHANT ACCOUNTS

Obviously, it's a lot easier for a consumer to place an order by credit card than by writing a check and mailing an order form. Therefore, to increase your sales by 80 percent or more, it is imperative that you obtain a merchant account. A merchant account allows you to receive and process credit card orders.

To be able to obtain a merchant account through your bank, you must have excellent credit. To be able to obtain a merchant account through a large processing firm, you need to have very good credit.

Perhaps you have bad credit or perhaps you don't want to set up your own Web site, open a merchant account, and provide fulfillment? Do not despair. You can still list your e-books for sale online elsewhere. (See Chapters 10 and 11 for details.) You just don't get to keep 100 percent of your proceeds. The good part about not doing your own fulfillment is that you can spend more time marketing your book and less time on bookkeeping and processing orders.

You can find hundreds of merchant account providers online by searching your favorite search engine for the term "merchant account." I use CardService International (*www.cardservice.com*). Beware of shady spam (junk e-mail) promoting merchant account services. Don't ever use merchant services that send you spam. If they need to rely on spam to sell their services, you should not share your customers' credit card information with them.

Merchant accounts consist of the following:

Purchase/Lease of Software

I purchased the software I use to process credit card transactions for $600. However, you can lease the software for around $40 per month. You will probably have to sign a two-year lease.

Discount Rate

This term discount rate is confusing. You don't get a discount. In fact, no one gets a discount. The discount rate is the amount discounted from a transaction to pay the credit card firm. The standard discount rate usually ranges from 3 to 5 percent or more depending on what credit card your customer is using. For example, if your customer makes a $10 purchase using his American Express card and the discount is 5 percent, American Express will keep 5 percent of that purchase ($0.50). If your customer makes a $100 purchase, American Express will take $5.

I know these varying percentages seem high, but if you consider the considerable increase in sales that your merchant account will bring, you will realize that taking credit cards is imperative for your business to survive.

Per Transaction Fees

You will be charged a set fee for each transaction you process. I pay $0.30 per transaction. If I process two hundred sales in a month, my transaction fees are $60.

Monthly Minimum

Most merchant firms require a monthly minimum of $25 for combined discount rates and transaction fees.

Statement Fee

The statement fee is for administrative charges associated with the firm's processing of your transactions, around $10 per month.

Authorization Gateway Fee

You will need to pay an authorization gateway fee of about $20 per month for access to the authorization servers processing your transactions.

Totals

So, if I sold two hundred books last month totaling $3,000, my total merchant account expenses would be $205.

Equipment/software lease: $40

Statement fee: $10

Discount (average 2.5 percent): $75.00

Transaction fees (200 @ .30): $60.00

Gateway fees: $20.00

Again, this might seem steep, but keep in mind that 80 percent of my sales would not have occurred had I not accepted credit cards. I would have only made a $600 profit instead of a $2,795 profit.

When you apply for a merchant account, you will receive an application, similar to a credit card application. You'll be required to divulge your credit history and details about your business. Your merchant service will deposit the funds for your sales directly into your bank account within two to three business days.

When I opened my business bank account, I paid $11 at the local courthouse, obtained my DBA certificate, drove to the bank, presented my certificate, and my account was opened, all in the space of one hour. The merchant account, however, took about three days to activate after the paperwork was complete.

Once your merchant account is active, your books are stacked in the garage (if you've printed them), and your e-book is ready to sell, you'll be in business! If you're the organized sort, this should all be pretty simple for you: take orders, process orders, and make sure each customer is happy and that your bank account is even happier.

INCOMING ORDERS

My merchant account software e-mails me every time an order comes through. For fast reference, I keep a spreadsheet in Microsoft Excel of all processed orders. This is imperative in the event a customer can't remember what they ordered later or if you need to credit someone's credit card for something. Don't assume your merchant account service is tracking orders for you. They do keep logs, but they will be of no use to you from a customer service standpoint.

I also save every electronic transaction. When my e-mailbox grows heavy with orders, I move them to a disk and save them. If a customer contests a charge later, you will need to be able to verify that they actually placed that charge. It's sad, but some people contest every charge made to their credit card just to get things without paying for them. Save every piece of evidence from every order for at least six months, but don't ever keep a customer's credit card information on your computer. It's too easy for hackers to come in and steal this information when you're online.

"SHIPPING" E-BOOKS

While electronic distribution of e-books can be confusing to those of us with limited technical knowledge, it's not as hard as you think. I distribute my e-books in three ways: direct consumer download, e-mail attachment, and by mail on CD-ROM.

Customer Download

If you have your own Web site (see Chapter 12 for tips on creating one) that enables you to transfer files to a server, you can set up your e-books to be downloaded by your buyers. The trick is simple. You can upload your e-book as a zip file. Zip files are compressed. With most Web browsers, when a Web site address with a suffix of .zip appears, the browser knows the file must be downloaded. It then asks the buyer where they want the file to go on their hard drive.

If you use Windows, converting just about any type of document to a zip file is a breeze. First, you must have Winzip, a shareware program that can be downloaded at *www.winzip.com*. Chances are you already have Winzip on your computer. Winzip zips and unzips (compresses and decompresses) computer files.

Once you've downloaded Winzip, open your Windows Explorer program. Find the directory your document is in, click once with your mouse to highlight the document file, and then click the right button on your mouse. A little window will pop up. One of the options will be "Add to zip." Click that. Your system will then create a zip file out of the document and it will instantly appear in the same directory, with a suffix of .zip. Now, if you're really 'Net savvy, upload your new, zipped e-book to your Web site's server. Now, when someone types in the URL where your e-book resides on the server (with its file extension of .zip, of course), their computer will ask them where they want the file to be downloaded to on their own computer. It's that simple!

The sample e-book I created in MSWord was converted to a zip file within seconds. If you want to see how it works, download our sample e-book at *www.booklocker.com/sampleebook.zip*. Read the messages your computer gives you to learn how the process will work for your customers.

If you want to implement passwords and instant delivery of your e-books when customers order, you'll need to either hire someone to perform the system setup for you, or you'll need to learn some more advanced HTML commands. My hosting service has a really good how-to page online that anyone can access. It's at: *www.web2010.com/support.html*.

E-mail Attachments

Delivering e-books as e-mail attachments offers less security, but is much easier to implement. As long as your book is less than one meg in size, your readers shouldn't experience problems receiving your book by e-mail.

I set up specific "delivery" e-mail messages for each of my books. Here's an example of instructions for opening a PDF e-book that is e-mailed to a customer.

FROM: YOU@YOUREMAILADDRESS.COM

TO: YOUR CUSTOMER@THEIREMAIL.COM

SUBJECT: DELIVERY: TITLE OF YOUR BOOK

THANK YOU FOR ORDERING FROM YOURWEBSITE.COM.

PLEASE FIND ATTACHED:

QTY: 1

PRODUCT: E-BOOK

TITLE OF YOUR BOOK
BY AUTHOR

EBOOKS ARE ZIPPED

ALL ITEMS ARE ZIPPED. PC USERS NEED WINZIP WHICH CAN BE DOWNLOADED FOR FREE AT:

HTTP://WWW.WINZIP.COM/DOWNLOADED.HTM

MAC USERS NEED A DECOMPRESSION PROGRAM AS WELL SUCH AS STUFFIT EX-PANDER WHICH CAN BE DOWNLOADED FOR FREE HERE:

HTTP://WWW.ALADDINSYS.COM/EXPANDER/EXPANDER MAC LOGIN.HTM!

PDF DOCUMENTS

EBOOKS ARE IN .PDF FORMAT. IF YOU DO NOT ALREADY HAVE ADOBE ACROBAT READER VERSION 4.0 (IT'S FREE), DOWNLOAD IT HERE:

HTTP://WWW.ADOBE.COM/PRODINDEX/ACROBAT/READSTEP.HTM#READER

IF YOU DO NOT HAVE THE MOST RECENT VERSION OF THE READER (4.0), YOU NEED TO DELETE YOUR CURRENT VERSION AND THEN DOWNLOAD VERSION 4.0 AT THE URL ABOVE. IF YOU DON'T DELETE THE OLD VERSION, YOU WILL EXPERI-ENCE PROBLEMS.

THEN, OPEN ADOBE ACROBAT READER, CLICK ON FILE, OPEN, AND FIND WHERE YOU SAVED THE EBOOK(S) YOU DOWNLOADED ABOVE.

IF YOU NEED HELP, CONTACT YOU@YOUREMAILADDRESS.COM

After addressing this e-mail message (which I have saved and used over and over again) to my customer, I attach my e-book file to the e-mail message. Then I click Send.

About 99 percent of my readers are able to follow these simple delivery instructions. The more complicated you make your transactions, the more time you'll spend trying to walk your buyers through the process. Be sure to make the opening and reading of your e-books as easy as possible. If one of your customers spends an hour trying to figure out how to read what you've sold to them, they will not order from you again.

Every e-mail program is different, but most of them have the option to attach a file to an e-mail message. Consult your e-mail program's Help option if needed.

CD-ROM

Ah, the lifeblood for those buyers who absolutely *must* have a physical product in their hands to feel fulfilled. We process perhaps a dozen CD-

ROM orders every day. For each CD-ROM, we simply charge each reader an additional $10 on top of the list price of the downloadable e-book. The $10 includes shipping and handling fees.

If you don't want to burn (create) your own CD-ROMs, you can order book burning from BookBurners.com (*www.bookburners.com*). Prices range from $3.50 to $6.00 each, depending on the quantity ordered. If you want to burn your own books on CD-ROM, you'll need to buy a CD-ROM burner. A decent one costs around $400. You will also need to buy CD-ROM labels and jewel cases (the clear plastic cases in which CD-ROMs are sold).

Burning CD-ROMs isn't difficult, but every burner is different. We burn three files on every CD-ROM: the actual e-book, the Adobe Acrobat Reader program (it is freely distributable), and a readme file that shows buyers how to read their e-books. The readme file contains an end-user license agreement (spelling out the copyright terms to the buyer), instructions on opening and reading the e-book, and even additional promotional material. Your readme file should be text-only or an HTML file so both PC and Macintosh owners can read it.

FULFILLING PHYSICAL ORDERS

I run my entire publishing business from my bedroom. This is, needless to say, hectic at times. As I look around me right now, I see four huge, towering sets of shelves, each piled high with blank CD-ROMs, books, boxes, blank mailing labels and CD-ROM labels, stamps, a postage scale, packing tape, and more. The shelf directly to my left is also stacked with candy wrappers. Hey, I write better when I'm chewing.

Every order I receive comes by e-mail, even those arriving from Amazon.com and Barnes & Noble. Orders that require a product to be physically mailed in return are printed and put in my "outgoing orders" box. Every Friday I print labels, stuff envelopes and boxes, and take a trip to the post office. This is, by far, the least enjoyable thing I do all week. But sales of physical products (print and CD-ROM books) are hot these days. I can easily ship a thousand dollars worth of products every Friday to Amazon.com and individual customers. So the money helps ease the clerical pains of the tasks.

10

SOFTWARE FOR THE INDEPENDENT PUBLISHER

Alan Canton

There are two ways to fail as an independent publisher. The first is to not sell enough books. The second is to sell too many . . . without having a business infrastructure to take care of all the drudge work of entering the orders and counting the money.

Every publisher needs some kind of a back-office software program for three basic reasons: efficiency, finance, and taxes.

You can't run a successful publishing company on three-by-five cards or an Excel spreadsheet. Even a small publisher needs a software program that will allow them to not spend their entire day doing paperwork. Time is money, and the more time taken to do drudge work, the less time there is for the important things like marketing, new book development, and publicity.

A good software system will allow you, the publisher, to have an idea of what kind of profit you are making or how big a loss you are taking. An end-of-month summary showing which titles are moving and which are not is an invaluable business tool.

And then there are sales taxes to pay and report. No more needs to be said about the complexity of local, state, and federal taxes and how software can help. Being able to click a button and total all of your taxable sales will save many days of mind-numbing work.

In deciding on what software to buy, the first rule is that price is not the best indicator of value. There are some expensive programs that are very good and there are some that are not. That is to be expected. But it is also true (and unexpected) that there are some low-priced packages that are every bit as good as those that cost much more.

The prime difference between a system costing a hundred dollars and one costing five thousand dollars is what are called "bells and whistles," extra features that some publishers need, but which will probably go unused by others. An example would be a subscription feature that would be valued by publishers who send out newsletters but useless to those who don't.

The bottom line is that all of the popular packages on the market, from the low-priced SOHO-123 to the premium-priced systems like Accumen, have the same basic features. There are modules (sections or categories in the software program) to enter vendors, products, customers, and order items. There are modules to accept payments and to print invoices or packing slips. And there are reports, reports, and more reports; the more expensive the program (usually), the more reports that can be generated. But regardless of price, the basic features are the same.

When the question arises of which non-basic features are important, the answer mainly depends on the buyer's particular needs. For example, all software programs will figure the tax for an order. But does the program allow the tax to be computed at the line item, if some items are taxable and some are not? For example, shipping is taxable in some areas and not in others.

A small publisher also needs to decide if their software should have integrated standard double-entry (credit/debit) accounting. While large integrated packages were in vogue up to a few years ago, today most business owners like to use a standard financial package such as Quicken, Medlin, or QuickBooks. The newer programs on the market have the ability to export necessary data to these inexpensive packages. While integration can have advantages, many publishers don't want to be locked into both an order-entry system and a finance system from a single vendor. Besides, many publishers have no need for a complex, top-heavy accounting system and find that a single entry method like the Medlin or Quicken serves their needs quite well.

Exporting of data may not seem like an important feature, but it is. For example, many Windows-based programs can export credit card transactions to the popular merchant programs like PC Authorize and IC Verify. And it is often necessary to export customer data for use in generating form letters and personalized marketing materials.

Every business wants reports, and here is where the greatest difference is between low-cost programs and the higher-priced ones. But the sheer number of reports should not be the determining factor of what system you purchase. Does the software output the reports that are necessary for you to run your publishing business? Some firms really need to output customer statements and aging reports. Others never use these but spend a lot of time analyzing sales summary reports. An important feature to look for is the ability to create your own report queries, reports you design yourself by choosing the specific information you want to consolidate and print.

Your software is of limited use if it is difficult to learn. The look and feel of a program should be a very important consideration.

It is important to be able to try the software before you buy it. Many packages are sold right over the Internet, where users have the ability to install it, work with it for a number of days, and either buy it or erase it.

Finally, the independent publisher needs to look into what kind of support they will get from the software vendor. This is where references are so valuable. While many references will say they like the program's features, make sure you question the references obtained from the vendor on the quality of the technical support. It is even better to find users on your own and not those supplied by the vendor. No vendor will give you dissatisfied clients to call! Also, call their customer or technical support before you buy. Ask some questions and see how they respond.

No off-the-shelf software package is perfect. If you want perfection, you will need to hire a programming staff (or contractors) and have a package created that will fill your exact needs. While most packages boast that they will do everything you want, what is closer to the truth is that most packages will do 100 percent of what you *need* done and about 90 percent of what you *want* done. The other 10 percent will cost from $100 to $10,000 extra.

You can download free trial versions of most of the software programs mentioned above at *download.cnet.com*.

Provided by Alan Canton of Adams-Blake Publishing (*www.adams-blake.com*), the creators of PUB123 and Sotto-123.

11

WHERE TO SELL YOUR PRINT AND CD-ROM BOOKS ONLINE

The large superstores won't give shelf space to single titles from small presses. (Well, your local bookstore might, but it's hard to get national distribution when you are self-published.) We don't recommend wasting your time trying to get distribution in bookstores until your book is selling in the thousands online.

Besides, who needs regular bookstores when there are so many thriving online bookstores? The top three online bookstores are increasingly happy to sell your print books as well as your self-published e-books.

We small publishers can now give the entire globe access to our products. Amazon.com's Advantage program truly levels the playing field for independent publishers and authors.

AMAZON.COM

Amazon.com should be your first stop. They have a program designed just for independent publishers: the Amazon.com Advantage program. It works on the consignment principle.

It turns out that while many people buying books online do look for books by title, many more search by key words and categories and read through multiple titles to see what's available. (In fact, it was in just this way that M. J.'s *Lip Service* was discovered by an editor at the Doubleday Book Club and Literary Guild.)

With the Advantage program, your book will always be "available within 24 hours." This is important because you don't want to lose impulse purchases. If a book isn't readily available, a customer might not want to wait.

Some publishers complain about the 55 percent share the Advantage program asks off the cover price of your book. But when you add up all the extras they offer, that difference will no longer be an issue.

They'll scan your cover, stock your book, and give you access to a current database to show how many books you've sold and how much they owe you. And working with them is so simple! Your book gets its own page that looks no different from John Grisham's or Alice Hoffman's books.

And the reader reviews at Amazon.com matter. You can quote them on your book cover and in any advertising or press releases that you send out. Surf here for more details on the Amazon.com Advantage program: *www.amazon.com/exec/obidos/subst/associates/join/associates.html*.

If you want to be listed on Amazon.com, but don't want them to take 55 percent of your cover price, you can sign up under their regular program. However, be warned that they won't stock your book under this program. The result is that your page on Amazon.com will say your book is available in four to six weeks rather than next-day delivery. This may very well hurt your sales in the long run. To learn more about Amazon.com's regular program, see *www.amazon.com/exec/obidos/subst/partners/publishers/publishers.html/102-5689837-3232845*.

BARNES&NOBLE.COM

Barnes&Noble.com (listed as *www.barnesandnoble.com* and *www.bn.com*) is a bit more elusive in providing information to publishers and self-published authors about getting listed. But their terms are similar to Amazon.com's. Surf here for their publisher FAQ: *www.bn.com/help/b_ faq.asp*.

Barnes & Noble recently started stocking books from small presses in their warehouse and are currently building a program similar to Amazon's Advantage Program. Send an e-mail to *availability@bn.com* to inquire about having your book stocked in their warehouse.

BORDERS.COM

Borders lists books on their site when they receive notification of new books registered at R. R. Bowker, the U.S. ISBN agency. You can no longer simply list your book's information with Borders.com. Once your book is listed on their site, you can request book page changes and updates by sending an e-mail to *corrections@Borders.com*.

If you have an ISBN and have registered your book with R. R. Bowker, your book may already appear at Borders.com.

THOUSANDS MORE

There are literally thousands of online bookstores you can find by using a search engine. We have provided a list of search engines in Part III. Spend some serious time going to online bookstore sites, and match your title to the stores that specialize in specific genres. There are how-to-bookstores, Christian inspirational bookstores, music, math, and madness bookstores, witchcraft bookstores, romance bookstores, and many more. If you can think of a category, you can find some online bookstores that will be more than happy to offer your book to their visitors.

12

E-PUBLISHERS AND PRINT-ON-DEMAND PUBLISHING

Many authors can't fathom stuffing their books in envelopes, running to the post office, or even e-mailing e-books and processing credit card charges. If you don't mind sharing some of your wealth with independent firms, then working with an e-publisher or print-on-demand (POD) publisher might be just what you're looking for.

New e-publishers enter the market every day. E-books are hot and everybody wants a piece of the pie. Unfortunately, most will try to take a huge piece of *your* pie (your book).

Like traditional publishers, many e-publishers have specific submission guidelines. Some e-publishers are more like e-bookstores. They publish anything and everything coming over the e-transom. Beware when working with these firms because the quality of their inventory may be so questionable that you might not want your book to be associated with them.

The business of working with an e-publisher is not so different from working with a traditional publisher, except don't hold your breath for an advance. Advances from e-publishers are rare and, when offered, may also come with a request for all rights.

WHAT THEY NEED

If the e-publisher screens incoming manuscripts, you will first be required to submit your book for consideration. If you are accepted for publication, you will receive specific guidelines for submitting your book to them. They may require your book to be in text-only format, or perhaps in Microsoft Word, PDF, or even HTML. Some e-publishers will create cover art for you while others will charge for it. Some will edit your book for you (usually for a fee), while others will insist that your book be professionally edited before you submit the final manuscript.

The e-publisher will also ask you to submit specific descriptive information so they can build a Web page for your book. You will submit key words that describe your book, a description, information about the author, and so on.

Once your book is online and available to the public, you will be able to refer potential buyers to your book's Web page that the e-publisher has built. Readers will then be able to click on your book, submit their credit card information, and click to order. The reader will then be given download instructions to retrieve your book, or will receive it by e-mail or even by mail on a CD-ROM.

So where's your money? Some e-publishers pay authors on a monthly basis, but most pay quarterly depending on what the author's royalty balance is.

WHAT YOU GET IN RETURN

Once your book is online and for sale at an e-publisher, you have a "store front," or a place where you can refer readers to buy your book. You also have a place that accepts credit cards, sends you checks, and maintains the technical back end of fulfillment (sending the books to buyers). Having your book for sale online at an e-publisher means not needing to worry about the multiple aspects of the front end and back end of e-commerce. This leaves authors with more time to promote themselves.

Here are some things to look out for when signing contracts with e-publishers.

Quality Control

You don't want your book associated with e-publishers that have no quality control and a poor reputation. Beware of e-publishers with poorly designed Web sites, no instant delivery capabilities, no capacity to process credit card orders (yes, they're out there!), and no screening process for manuscripts. If anything you see on their Web site makes you uncomfortable, find another e-publisher for your book. Don't hesitate to ask for references. Better yet, jump on an online discussion list and ask other writers and authors what they've heard about the e-publishers you're considering working with.

Royalty Verification

An author we know had a bad experience with a so-called literary agent. The agent decided to list all his clients' books for sale as e-books on his site, thus making him an agent/e-publisher. (The warning signs should have started when that happened!) The author became suspicious when the agent stopped responding to her e-mails about sales of her book. She then tested the agent by asking thirty friends and relatives to order her book. Three months later, the agent wrote to tell her she wouldn't be receiving any royalties that quarter because there were no sales. After the author threatened a lawsuit, the rights to the book were returned to her, but she never did receive her money. Cases like this are occurring online, so beware.

How do you know if you're really being paid for all the sales of your book? Well, you don't. You're at the mercy of the honesty of the firm you're dealing with. And, let me tell you: Don't ever trust anyone when it comes to money. You have a right to question the accounting records of your e-publisher and the right to receive documentation to back up their claims.

Friends and Family Method

To test the sales of your book at the e-publishers you have chosen to work with, follow the example of the author above. Lots of authors do this now and it appears to be working. Have some friends or family members (with last names different from yours) order your book and forward their sales receipts to you. When your royalty statement appears, see if the sales appear on the statement. If they don't, e-mail the e-publisher and ask for a more detailed statement. You deserve this information. If they refuse to share your sales information, don't hesitate to terminate your contract with them.

Honest mistakes can be made, so don't accuse before asking what happened. Sometimes an author has had more than one author account set up by mistake. Sometimes the HTML code on the site is incorrect. If one sale doesn't appear on your royalty statement, it might be an accident. If multiple sales over several months don't appear . . . put on your armor.

To avoid being a victim, choose e-publishers that let authors check their accounts twenty-four hours a day online. This makes it possible to track your sales frequently to ensure you are receiving what is rightfully yours and to put a stop to any discrepancies or theft from day one. The good news is that unscrupulous e-publishers are hearing about these incidents of others being caught stealing royalties and they're having a hard time working around the friends and family method.

Contract Period

Most e-publishers require authors to sign a contract that binds them to the e-publisher for a specific period of time ranging from one to five years or more. We've even heard of contracts that have no time period and no termination clause. As of this writing, Booklocker.com, Angela's company, is the only non-exclusive e-publisher that allows instant contract termination with only an e-mail notification from authors. MightyWords makes authors wait only thirty days, which is more than fair. Most e-publishers, however, lock authors in for a year or more. A quick out clause in a contract is a helpful alternative for authors who have been contacted by a traditional print publisher.

Non-Exclusives

E-publishers requesting non-exclusive electronic rights allow authors to post and sell their books at other sites. Links below are to contract pages, where available. The contract terms listed were accurate as of this writing, but terms change frequently, so always read any contract carefully before you sign. Post your book for sale at as many non-exclusive e-publishers as you want! The more places you're listed, the more exposure your book receives!

Booklocker.com
www.booklocker.com
70 percent royalties on list price of e-books 100 pages or more
50 percent royalties on list price of e-booklets (fewer than 100 pages)
Non-exclusive rights
Pays monthly
Angela's company, Booklocker.com, lists books free but accepts less than thirty percent of submitted manuscripts for publication. Also offers print-on-demand.

Mightywords.com
www.mightywords.com

50 percent royalties
Charges authors $1 per month for every book listed
Non-exclusive rights
Pays quarterly
Monthly fee is automatically charged to your credit card

Erotic-Ebooks.com

www.erotic-ebooks.com
Erotic literature and nonfiction books dealing with sexuality
50 percent royalties
Non-exclusive rights
Pays monthly

PC Books, Inc.

www.pc-books.net
Charges $25 set-up fee
50 percent royalties
Non-exclusive rights
Pays quarterly

1st Books

www. 1stbooks.com /newbooks.htm
Charges substantial set-up fee (up to $500), but pays 100 percent royalties
    until that fee is "paid back" to the author.
30 percent royalties
Non-exclusive rights
Pays quarterly

Archetype-Press

www.archetype-press.com /contract.htm
For initial product upload, password, and editing privileges, charges $45
    for first 5,000 words, $75 for 5,000–30,000 words, $95 for manuscripts
    over 30,000 words. Also charges a $10 per month membership fee.

CyberNet Books

www.cybernetbooks.com /authorw.htm
Royalties not provided at Web site.
Non-exclusive, but authors may have to wait up to six months for con-
    tract termination.

PRINT-ON-DEMAND (POD) PUBLISHERS

A print-on-demand publisher creates a computer file of your book, complete with cover art, contents, and everything required to print your book. They store this computer file and use it later to print one copy of your book at a time, on demand. This saves the cost of thousands of dollars for a massive print run.

Authors are usually required to pay set-up fees to the POD firms (anywhere from $99 to several hundred dollars) and then receive a percentage of each sales transaction later. Like traditional publishers, some POD firms require authors to sign long-term contracts for their services and also request specific print and electronic rights to the book. Authors are often required to refer all sales for print versions of their books to their POD firm. In return, the author earns royalties of around 20 percent. Authors must purchase their own print books, they do receive them at a discount, but royalties are usually extinguished in these transactions, of course. Similar to traditional publishing, authors are usually paid on a quarterly, biannual, or annual basis.

Some POD firms offer print and electronic book publishing and pay anywhere from 20 to 50 percent royalties on these transactions. Beware, however, of the rights issues involved. We've heard of POD firms forcing authors to buy copies of their own e-books to distribute to book reviewers. This is ludicrous considering the fact that the cost to manufacture multiple e-books, after the initial book is complete, is nil.

Exclusive publishing rights means all sales of your books must go through this firm. You will have to refer all buyers to that publishing company's Web site, even for sales of the electronic version of your book (if the POD firm has asked for electronic rights). Some of these contracts can be terminated upon written request, but there is usually a waiting period. This could potentially hurt the author if a major print publisher wants a contract but must wait until the rights from the POD publisher revert back to the author. Many traditional publishers won't wait for this and will rescind their offer.

One firm that has a non-exclusive rights arrangement is Xlibris (*www.xlibris.com*). Xlibris is partially owned by Random House Ventures. Another major player in this type of service is iUniverse (*www.iuniverse. com*). The least expensive package is $99. However, their contract specifies exclusive rights, including electronic rights. If you want to terminate your contract, you can, but you might have to wait a year to get your rights back.

Authors earn 20 percent royalties on print sales and 50 percent royalties on electronic sales. iUniverse.com is partially owned by Barnes & Noble.

Booklocker.com offers POD as well and allows authors to purchase their own books at a discount. Authors can then sell their books from their own Web sites and other venues. Booklocker.com requests non-exclusive rights on POD contracts, and authors can terminate their contracts at any time. Royalties for POD books are 35 percent, the highest in the industry.

13

WEB SITES FOR AUTHORS

Every author should have a Web site, and building one, designing it, and maintaining it can be as simple or as complicated as you want it to be. You can do it for free or dive right in and pay thousands of dollars to a professional Web design firm. In any case, a Web site creates a place for readers to learn about a book, interact with its author, and, finally, provides ordering information for that all-important purchase.

FREE WEB SITES

Most beginners build their own Web sites using one of the free site services online. Popular ones are Tripod (*www.tripod.com*) and Geocities (*www.geocities.com*). These sites are very easy to use. You can build a Web site with a few clicks of your mouse and there is no cost to keep it on their server. However, you won't have your own domain name. Your domain will instead be something like *www.tripod.lycos.com/yoursite.html*.

If you want to go all out and do it right, buy your own domain name and get to work learning HTML. There are many software programs available that make learning HTML quite simple, including FrontPage (*www.microsoft.com/frontpage*) and Homesite. You can also download a trial version of Homesite by typing the word "homesite" in the search box at *download.cnet.com*.

You can choose a domain name and, if it's not already taken, buy it here: *www.networksolutions.com*.

Your Web site will need to sit on a server somewhere. This is where the Web hosting firms come in. Web2010 (*www.web2010.com*) charges about $20 per month to host your Web site. You can buy your domain name directly from them as well. Their servers almost never go down, and they offer a wonderful support team and a variety of services for even the most basic accounts. Web sites come complete with e-mail addresses, secure servers (for credit card transactions), and even a built-in search engine for your Web site.

WEB SITE PROMOTION

It's one thing for an author to get a domain name and Web site, but quite another to build Web traffic and generate sales. It takes a whole separate set of promotional and marketing skills, and most authors are too busy writing books to take the time to learn all that.

AuthorsontheWeb.com (*www.authorsontheweb.com*), the brainchild of Carol Fitzgerald, president and CEO of The Book Report Network, is dedicated to doing just that—making an author's Web site speak to and motivate readers.

The Book Report Network has spent four years developing interactive magazine content for seven online sites including *www.bookreporter.com, www.teenreads.com,* and *www.kidsreads.com.* With over 2.5 million impressions (downloaded ad banners) and 400,000 dedicated book lovers, they've learned volumes about what those readers want and expect from authors.

"Until the Internet, authors had been viewed as inaccessible celebrities by their fans," said Fitzgerald. What she's learned is that the more a reader can reach out and touch an author through a Web site—and exchange questions and answers—the more likely that reader is to become an avid fan.

"Once they can interact with the author, the reader falls in love with them," said Fitzgerald who last year created a Web site for Janet Evanovich (*www.evanovich.com*) to help her communicate with her fans. "We found a twist to make the site work—having one of Evanovich's book characters interview her—and it took off!"

Charter pricing for AuthorsontheWeb.com starts as low as $300 for setup plus a $50-per-month maintenance fee, which is competitive with other sites such as *www.bookzone.com*. But Fitzgerald also offers packages with sophisticated marketing and interactive applications ranging from

$1,000 to $7,500. "But those sites are for bestselling authors whose sites need constant maintenance as well as hosting help," she said.

Bookzone.com, the brainchild of Mary Westheimer, is a very large site that hosts over 1,500 smaller sites. Not all of these are writing sites, but they all do, in one way or another, have something to do with the business of publishing.

Susie Bright, author of *Full Exposure* and editor of *Best American Erotica,* designed her own Web site (*www.susiebright.com*) in 1996 and gets between six thousand and nine thousand hits a day. She considers it one of the most important ways she can interact with her readers. "It's friendly, funny, and flirtatious and no one was more surprised than me by how many people keep coming back," said Bright. "I think it works because I give it as much attention as any other writing project."

An additional benefit to having an author's site is that it eliminates the need for a press kit (more on this topic in Part III). Bright sends all inquiries to her site, which offers far more information than she could ever send out in a printed folder.

Katherine Neville, bestselling author of *The Magic Circle,* started her Web site (*www.katherineneville.com*) in 1998 out of a need to deal with her abundance of fan mail—over 150 letters a week. "A secondary reason was that so many of my readers were interested in the research I do for my novels. My site gave me a way to share more of it with them." Now many of her fans send *her* valuable research she might not find any other way. "My site is immediate and it's hands-on, and I like having that relationship with my readers," she said.

You don't need to buy a domain name that is your name, per se. Many authors buy domain names that creatively label the genre they work in. One example of this is Nancy Hendrickson's Web site, AncestorNews.com (*www.ancestornews.com*). Nancy writes genealogy books and distributes an electronic genealogy newsletter to keep her readers coming back for more.

It's no secret that the way to build readership is for an author to establish a relationship with potential fans. But there's never before been a surefire way to do that other than national book tours, which are so time intensive and expensive that only the top bestselling authors do them regularly anymore. Web sites are not only an alternative to tours but, in a way, a solution to them.

14

THE BESTSELLING E-BOOKS ARE . . .

Angela Adair-Hoy

While many of the print bestsellers receiving all the hype are fiction, you can attain fame and wealth authoring a nonfiction book. Nonfiction how-to books are currently the bestselling e-books. Here are some lessons they can teach you about achieving success.

YOU MUST BE AN EXPERT IN YOUR FIELD

To have a successful nonfiction book, you must already be a recognized authority in the field you are writing about or must establish yourself as a new authority in that field. If the readers of your topic don't know who you are and what you've accomplished, they won't buy from you. While you can sometimes establish your credentials with a well-written "About the Author" section, it is better to spread the word about yourself in the communities that are interested in your topic. You need to let people know, "This is who I am and this is why you must buy my book!"

SHAMELESS SELF-PROMOTION WORKS

I am never shy about publishing my monthly book revenues in my ads. I want my readers to know what I've accomplished. They will then know that they can do it, too. When a member of the media called me one of the "most prolific and profitable self-published authors on the Internet today,"

I began posting the quote everywhere (after obtaining permission to use the quote, of course).

Never be afraid to share the story of your success. It's contagious! Never feel that what you have to say isn't worth reading. It is! Never be so humble as to make readers think your book isn't worth buying. Your self-confidence, or lack thereof, will show through in every piece of correspondence you write.

HOW-TO BOOKS ARE THE BESTSELLERS

Anyone buying a nonfiction book is buying to learn. Sometimes they want to learn about something. But most of the time they want to learn how to do something. And, of these how-to books, the how-to-make-money-doing-something books are the most sought-after and thus the most profitable.

SEX $ELLS

I have published a variety of how-to-books (written by other authors) on how-to writing topics. The most profitable, aside from my two e-publishing books, is *It's a Dirty Job . . . Writing Porn for Fun and Profit* by Katy Terrega (*www.writersweekly.com/index-dirtyjob.htm*). Did the writers buying this book really want to start submitting erotic literature to magazines? Perhaps. However, after reading personal comments from her readers, I realized that many of them wanted to taste a sample of her erotic fiction. After reading the book, many of them went to Erotic-Ebooks.com (*www.erotic-ebooks.com*) to purchase Katy's anthology of erotic short stories.

Yes, sex sells! Of the thousands of online books on the market, M. J. Rose's contemporary erotic novel, *Lip Service,* was the first to be grabbed by the major publishers.

So, do you still think you can't get rich and famous through self-publishing? Keep reading!

Part Two

SELF-PUBLISHING SUCCESS STORIES: IF THEY DID IT, SO CAN YOU!

15

SMALL PRESSES, BIG SUCCESSES

M. J. Rose

There are more than fifty-three thousand publishers in the United States. Of that number, there are a mere twenty-three large houses (such as Simon & Schuster, St. Martin's Press, and Random House). Each of these houses publishes more than five hundred titles a year.

There are only three hundred medium-size houses that publish fewer than five hundred titles a year.

The rest—over fifty-two thousand—are small presses that produce between one and thirty titles a year but account for over 30 percent of all books sold in the United States. That's a lot of books. And yet bookstores and the media still look askance at small publishing companies, putting them only a few steps above vanity presses.

It's an attitude that disturbs small publishers but certainly does not deter them. Against all odds, they continue to produce quality books that not only sell, but also often win prestigious awards and occasionally make it to the *New York Times* bestseller list.

Some of these publishers work out of their garages or kitchens. Some sell books out of the trunks of their cars. Some don't even sell their tomes outside of their own Web sites or online bookstores.

Few small publishers can afford the kind of publicity and advertising campaigns that are the norm for the big houses. Instead they do their own publicity, rely on word of mouth, do radio interviews, and use Internet newsgroups, listservs, and Web sites to get a buzz going.

- Dorothy Molstad of Waldman House Press has sold well over 1,250,000 copies of *A Cup of Christmas Tea* by Tom Hegg and Warren Hanson (illustrator), and 100,000 copies of *The Next Place,* written and illustrated by Warren Hanson. To sell books, Dorothy says, "I did a lot of Internet searching for local targets." One book received the Award of Merit at the Midwest Independent Publisher Awards.

- *Handbook to a Happier Life,* self-published by Jim Donovan of Bovan Publishing Group, has sold over 75,000 copies. "Essentially I did it— actually the book's content did it—by becoming clear as to who my target readers were and asking better questions to go about finding them. Most of my sales have been to the corporate market, sold in bulk."

- *Spring Cleaning for the Soul,* written by Joy Krause and published by Abbondanza! has sold over 15,000 copies in ten months. To promote her book, she has done over two hundred radio shows, as well as national and local TV shows.

- May T. Watts sold over 220,000 copies of *Tree Finder: A Manual for Identifying Trees by Their Leaves.*

- Diane Pfeifer has published three titles that have sold more than 20,000 each. They include *Gone with the Grits, Grits Bits,* and *The Pregnant Husband's Handbook.*

- More than 90,000 copies have been sold of *New Jersey Day Trips* by Barbara Hudgins.

- Tim McCormick, President of Greentree Publishing, has sold over 169,000 copies of *How to Behave So Your Children Will, Too* by Sal Severe, Ph.D. Over half of his sales were book club sales.

Each one of these stories defies convention. In spite of reviewers who rarely review a book unless they recognize the publisher's name, despite bookstores that are reluctant to order more than one or two copies of an independently published book, and notwithstanding prohibitive advertising costs, these publishers persevere and succeed. They succeed time and again by utilizing local newspapers, the Internet, and creative marketing plans.

The success of independent publishers speaks volumes about the power of entrepreneurial skills and determination. Bestseller status may elude them, but they are writing their own successes stories, one book at a time.

16

SELF-PUBLISHERS HALL OF FAME

John Kremer

Smaller than small presses are self-publishers. Yet some of these enterprising entrepreneurs have had giant successes. Here are some highlights from the "Self-Publishers Hall of Fame"; the complete list is updated frequently and posted online at *www.bookmarket.com/selfpublish.html*.

- Ken Blanchard and Spencer Johnson originally self-published *The One-Minute Manager* so they could sell the book for $15. This was at a time when all the experts were telling them that they'd never sell such a short book for such a high price. In a three-month period of time, they sold over 20,000 copies in the San Diego area alone—and then sold the reprint rights to William Morrow. The book launched a line of One-Minute books that have sold millions of copies. *The One-Minute Manager* itself has sold more than 12 million copies since 1982 and been published in more than twenty-five languages.
- Richard Bolles originally self-published *What Color Is Your Parachute?* Later he sold the rights to Ten Speed Press. The book has now spent over five years on the *New York Times* bestseller list and returns to the bestseller list each year when a new edition comes out. The book has sold well over 10 million copies thus far and has been published in fourteen languages.
- H. Jackson Brown originally self-published his *Life's Little Instruction Book*. Soon thereafter, the book was bought by Rutledge Hill, a local publisher who went on to sell more than 5 million copies. The book made the bestseller lists in both hardcover and paperback.

- Deepak Chopra vanity-published his first book and then sold the rights to Crown Publishing. The book went on to become the first of many bestsellers for this author.
- *No Thanks,* by e. e. cummings, was a volume of poetry financed by his mother. On the first page, he listed the thirteen publishers who had rejected the book, which became one of his classics.
- Ben Dominitz self-published several books, one on free travel (*Travel Free*) and another on romance, before establishing Prima Publishing, now one of the largest of the independent small publishers. In less than fifteen years, he built a company that has now published well over 1,500 titles, has more than 140 employees, and competes with the New York publishers on an equal standing. Prima has grown to a $60 million a year business. Their Prima Games division is the largest publisher of electronic and computer game books.
- In 1982, when his wife was expecting their third child, John Erickson borrowed $2,000 and self-published the first book in his *Hank the Cowdog* series. To make sales, he loaded his pickup with copies and sold them at cattle auctions, rodeos, schools, Rotary meetings, and anywhere else he could find a crowd. He later sold the rights to Gulf Publishing. Combined sales of his thirty novels are 3 million copies.
- Richard Paul Evans self-published his little holiday story, *The Christmas Box,* and sold thousands of copies in the Salt Lake City area. When the major publishers became interested in the book, dozens of them participated in a two-day auction. Simon & Schuster came out the winner. They only had to pay Evans a $4.2 million advance (which included the rights to a prequel as well). He retained the rights to his paperback edition. The next year, both editions landed on the bestseller lists.
- In hopes of getting another bestseller like those from the Delaney sisters, Warner Books paid ninety-eight-year-old Jessie Lee Brown Foveaux more than $1 million for the rights to her self-published reminiscences, *Any Given Day.*
- Les and Sue Fox self-published *The Beanie Baby Handbook* in 1997. By July of 1998, they had gone back to press eight times for an in-print total of 3 million copies, while the book established itself in the number two spot on the *New York Times* bestseller list (under advice, how-to, and miscellaneous). This is an example of a self-publisher taking a hot topic and running with it long before any larger publishers could get a book out.

- Benjamin Franklin, using the pen name of Richard Saunders, self-published his *Poor Richard's Almanack* in 1732 and continued to produce the almanac for another twenty-six years. Many of his famous sayings came from the almanac.
- After poet Nikki Giovanni sold 10,000 copies of her first self-published book, *Black Feeling Black Talk,* William Morrow offered her a contract for future books. Since then, they have sold more than 500,000 copies of eight volumes of poetry and five books of essays. Her most recent collection, *Love Poems,* dedicated to the late rapper Tupac Shakur, has sold more than 70,000 copies.
- L. Ron Hubbard originally self-published his book *Dianetics,* which founded a new church (Scientology) and has sold more than 20 million copies in the past forty-five years.
- John Javna self-published *50 Simple Things You Can Do to Save the Earth* just in time to catch the environmental awareness wave of the 1980s—and months before the major publishers came out with other ecology titles. His book got all the press and sold over 4.5 million copies.
- Vicky Lansky sold 300,000 copies of her self-published parenting title, *Feed Me, I'm Yours,* and then sold the rights to Bantam Books, which went on to sell 8 million copies of that title and millions of copies of her other books. That first book helped to establish Meadowbrook Press, now operated by her ex-husband, and Book Peddlers, Vicky's publishing firm, which republishes her books after the big publishers let them go out of print, along with new titles written by other authors as well as herself.
- Joanna Lund self-published her *Healthy Exchanges Cookbook* after going from 300 pounds and a size 28 to 170 pounds and a size 14, using the low-fat recipes collected in the book. After selling 150,000 copies through her own promotional efforts, she sold the reprint rights to Putnam for a six-figure advance. Several books later, Joanna is now the cookbook queen of QVC, having sold more books via the home shopping network than any other author. She also runs a multimillion-dollar enterprise that includes a PBS cooking show, a catalog, and a newsletter.
- Everyone told Sandra Haldeman Martz that collections of short stories and poetry don't sell, especially if written by unknown women. But she didn't listen. She self-published *When I Am an Old Woman, I Shall Wear Purple,* which went on to sell more than 4 million copies, inspiring Purple Parties nationwide for women hitting the age of fifty. It was

then chosen as book of the year by the American Booksellers Association. With her publishing company, Papier-Mâché Press, Sandra went on to publish many other titles for women.

- Marlo Morgan self-published *Mutant Message Down Under,* sold 370,000 copies and, once it began to take off, sold the rights to HarperCollins for $1.7 million. Foreign rights were sold to fourteen countries.

- Richard Nixon self-published one of his books, *Real Peace.*

- Tim O'Reilly, president of O'Reilly & Associates, started out as a self-publisher of books on UNIX. He now runs the fourth largest trade computer book publisher, which grew out of his self-publishing efforts.

- Tom Peters self-published *In Search of Excellence* and sold more than 25,000 copies directly to consumers in the first year. Then Warner Books published a new edition, which has gone on to sell more than 10 million copies.

- Jo Petty paid a vanity press to publish the first printing of *Apples of Gold.* When that printing of 7,500 copies sold out in three months, she wasn't willing to finance another printing. A few years later, in 1965, she sold the rights to C. R. Gibson Company, a gift and stationery company. Over the next twenty years, 3.7 million copies were sold. Even now, the book sells about 85,000 copies every year. The book, which became the foundation for the C. R. Gibson book publishing operation, established books as gifts. *Apples of Gold* has never been reviewed, never been advertised, never sold to a book club, and never sold through direct mail.

- James Redfield sold over 80,000 copies of his self-published book, *The Celestine Prophecy,* from the trunk of his car. He then sold the reprint rights to Warner Books for $800,000. The book has gone on to sell 5.5 million copies.

- Irma Rombauer used $3,000 from her husband's estate to self-publish *The Joy of Cooking* in 1931. Since then, this cookbook has sold millions of copies. Sixty-six years later, it still sells more than 100,000 copies per year. In November 1997, Scribners published a completely revised fifth edition, the first new edition in twenty years. By early December, the book had already made the bestseller lists with more than 750,000 copies in print.

- In 1918, William Strunk self-published *The Elements of Style* for his college classes at Cornell University. The book was later revised by E. B. White and continues to sell thousands of copies every year.

- Henry David Thoreau originally self-published *Walden,* an American classic that sells thousands of copies every year—even now, more than one hundred years after his death!
- Mark Twain self-published *The Adventures of Huckleberry Finn* when he got tired of the foolishness of his previous publishers.
- Walt Whitman self-published many editions of his collected poems, *Leaves of Grass.* While he didn't get wealthy from self-publishing, he did become known as America's poet.
- K. J. A. Wishnia self-published her first mystery novel, *23 Shades of Black,* which was nominated for Edgar and Anthony awards. She sold the rights to her second novel, *Soft Money,* to Dutton. HBO aired a series based on her first novel, produced by Spike Lee's 40 Acres and a Mule Filmworks.
- Tim and Nina Zagat self-published their first Zagat Survey in 1979. By 1998, their *Zagat New York Survey* alone sold more than 600,000 copies. In addition, they now publish thirty-five other surveys covering Los Angeles, San Francisco, Boston, Chicago, Washington, D.C., London, Paris, and other cities.

Other successful self-publishers include William Blake, Edgar Rice Burroughs, Stephen Crane, Mary Baker Eddy, Zane Grey, James Joyce, Rudyard Kipling, D. H. Lawrence, Anaïs Nin, Thomas Paine, Edgar Allan Poe, Ezra Pound, Carl Sandburg, George Bernard Shaw, Upton Sinclair, Gertrude Stein, and Virginia Woolf.

John Kremer, author of *1001 Ways to Market Your Books,* helps authors get their books on the bestseller lists (*www.bookmarket.com/self-publish.html*).

17

WHEN E-PUBLISHING WORKS BETTER THAN PRINT

Nancy Hendrickson

E-PUBLISH!

I've been interested in my family's history for most of my life. When I was a kid, my grandmother told me stories about teaching in a one-room schoolhouse, and about her own father's birth during a Civil War raid. I grew up with genealogy in my blood.

With the availability of genealogical information on the Internet, returning to my childhood love of family history was a natural step. Although I've been online since 1986, the explosion in Internet genealogy has only been a recent trend. In fact it became so popular that *Time* magazine did a cover issue on "cyber-roots."

As an author, and a genealogist, I knew the time was perfect to write a book that combined my love of genealogy with my thirteen-plus years of online experience.

I had already written two books, both of which were published by a traditional publishing company. My experience with them was—to be honest—less than satisfactory. Once the books were published, I had no control or input on marketing and, in the book business, marketing is the name of the game.

When I decided to write an Internet genealogy book, I wasn't sure I wanted to approach a publishing company. However, I wanted to explore all my options.

First, I could go mainstream. This means writing a proposal and sample chapters and submitting them to a publishing company. After months of waiting, I'd be given a thumbs-up or thumbs-down. If a thumbs-up, I'd receive little or no advance and have absolutely no control or influence on what marketing methods the publishing company used.

Second, I could self-publish the book. In self-publishing, I could either have a printing company print the book, or I could go "cheap and dirty" by Xeroxing copies of the book and have the copy shop bind them. In either case, I'd be in total control of sales and marketing. This option held some appeal, but I knew I'd be looking at a $1,000 investment at least. Although this option was more attractive than going mainstream, it had its drawbacks.

Third, I could write the book, then sell it as an electronic document. If I went electronic, I had no overhead costs, no postage, and I retained the ability to market the book as aggressively as possible. Additionally, when second and third editions of the book were released, I could easily make the editorial changes in an electronic document.

My choice was obvious. I was going to become an electronic publisher. Now all I had to do was write the book!

Writing *How to Find More Ancestors Through Online Networking* was a breeze. I organized all of the information I'd been collecting over the past few years and structured it into a book format. I focused on this particular facet of Internet genealogy because it is an area in which I've had tremendous success.

By networking with other Internet genealogists, I've added thousands of names to my own family database and met cousins I never knew existed. This is exciting stuff for a family researcher, and I wanted to share my successful strategies with my readers.

I quickly finished writing the book and then sent a press release to a few editors of Internet genealogy newsletters. In the first week my electronic book was available, I made over $600! I was shocked. This amount was more than the total amount I earned from my other two print books combined! I've continued to earn money from this book at a steady rate. If you're interested in climbing the family tree, you can order a copy at *www.ancestornews.com*.

In the two months since the book's release, I've already added two new chapters and made several changes, including the addition of several family photos as illustrations. One of the great advantages of electronic publishing is the ability to fill your book with as many full-color photos as you want.

In traditional publishing, using photographs is tremendously expensive, causing many books to be under-illustrated. This is never a worry for the e-publisher.

The feedback from readers has been uplifting. One wrote to tell me how the book had inspired her to renew her efforts in searching for her family; another told me my suggestions had given him a brand-new research strategy and it was already paying off. Getting this kind of instant feedback, along with having a financially successful product, feels great!

I'm now preparing an electronic book on the hows and whys of collecting. It's filled with articles on how to become a savvy collector, whether your shelves are lined with marbles, *Star Wars* characters, or Elvis memorabilia. Be looking for it on the Net.

From the very first day I logged onto an online service back in 1986, I knew the electronic world was the place I wanted to be. The ability to communicate instantly and worldwide appealed to me in a way that few could understand. Now, as an electronic publisher, I can reach that worldwide audience quicker and cheaper than any print-based company, and I can deliver my product instantly via e-mail.

I'm living proof that electronic publishing is an author's dream.

Nancy Hendrickson is the author of *How to Find More Ancestors Through Online Networking*. She is Webmaster at *www.ancestornews.com*.

18

SELLING ON A SHOESTRING

Shel Horowitz

The Internet, and my diversified presence online (not just a three hundred-fifty plus–page Web site but also active participation on many lists and constant attention to my e-mail), has brought many benefits to me as a writer and publisher.

Among the most interesting: I sold a copy of *Marketing Without Megabucks: How to Sell Anything on a Shoestring* to a fellow in Germany who visited my site in 1996. Three years later, he asked if the book was available in German; he wanted to give a copy to everyone who worked for him. Since it's not available, he is exploring translating it himself. He used two chapters in the book to build a million-dollar business with no advertising expense. I used this testimonial to draft and send a press release (and post it on my site at *www.frugalfun.com/germantestimonial.html*). It is now the lead item in my press packet promoting that book. The ensuing months brought some excellent publicity, including a three-page spread in *Bottom Line/Business.* Not bad for a title written eight years ago!

In fact, the Internet allowed me to keep the book current by including a substantial update via e-mail. This lets me charge about 40 percent above the original cover price. It also kept otherwise obsolete inventory alive until I replaced it with an all-new book, *Grassroots Marketing: Getting Noticed in a Noisy World* (Chelsea Green, 2000). I've been selling this book steadily over the Net since its release.

Other ways the Net helps my writing and publishing career:

- Book sales at the full retail price plus shipping
- Media inquiries, including the BBC
- Lots of marketing clients who want press releases written and other services (my main livelihood—I'm a part-time publisher and full-time writer)
- Article reprint sales, purchased from my Web site, and new assignments
- A small amount of direct advertising revenue
- Lots and lots of exposure for my books and services, through the distribution of monthly tipsheets that only take about half an hour a month to write
- Unlimited space for marketing materials. For both *The Penny-Pinching Hedonist: How to Live Like Royalty with a Peasant's Pocketbook* and my marketing books, I post the table of contents, reader/press quotes, the cover, and several excerpts along with sales materials.
- An easy-to-remember "leave behind" for radio listeners: My URL, *www.frugalfun.com,* with a reason to visit. And far more radio/TV coverage, mostly arranged through GuestFinder.com (see Chapter 51 for more information about their services).
- Feedback on publishing-industry vendors/practices

Cyberspace has taken our two-person home business in rural Massachusetts and turned it into an international business. I have sold books in over a dozen countries and have marketing clients in the United Kingdom, Belgium, and Cyprus, as well as throughout the United States.

Shel Horowitz is author of *Grassroots Marketing: Getting Noticed in a Noisy World* and author/publisher of *Marketing Without Megabucks: How to Sell Anything on a Shoestring* and *The Penny-Pinching Hedonist: How to Live Like Royalty with a Peasant's Pocketbook.* He is Webmaster at *www.frugalfun.com,* offering articles on how to save money, run a business better, and have more fun.

19

INTERNET PUBLISHING . . .
A MIDLIST AUTHOR'S DREAM

Pauline Baird Jones

When I was a kid, I hated that story about *The Little Engine That Could.* Adults were always trotting it out when they wanted me to do something I knew I didn't want to start, let alone finish. But it became my mantra when I ran into a brick wall known in publishing as the Midlist Crunch.

The midlist (all books not considered bestsellers), where most first-time novelists make their publication debut, was shrinking as publishing houses merged and closed imprints. Even worse, the romantic suspense genre I loved and wrote in was considered dead on arrival on most New York editorial desks.

It wasn't easy to realize that I could work hard, perfect my craft, submit to everyone in New York and their dog, and still not make it into publication.

Then I discovered that the midlist wasn't actually shrinking, it was moving to the Internet. With that move, there are expanded and exciting new opportunities for authors. Two years ago I took my books directly to readers via a small electronic press and the Internet.

When my first book, *Pig in a Park,* was electronically released and then nominated for a Reviewer's Choice Award from *Romantic Times* magazine (alongside such industry heavyweights as Linda Howard and Stella Cameron), I was able to contract for the e-rights to my second book, *The Last Enemy,* in just under twenty-four hours by e-mail.

With this double publishing credit on my résumé, I submitted it to Books in Motion (*www.booksinmotion.com*), who released an unabridged audio edition of *Pig in a Park* in September of 1999. Around the same time,

Fictionworks (*www.fictionworks.com*) came to me and contracted for the audio rights to *The Last Enemy*.

That double publication credit helped me pitch both books to Thorndike Press, who offered contracts for the hardcover rights.

Because *Pig* and *Enemy* were getting so much attention, I contracted my third book in half an hour via e-mail. It is presently undergoing a title change, but at this writing is known as *Do Wah Diddy . . . Die* and will be the launch book of Starlight Writer Publications' new romantic comedy line, Sunlight Romances.

The script adaptation of this book was optioned by IndieGal Productions after an e-mail pitch where I used my publication credits to boost my résumé, and it is now scheduled to go into production. When the press release about this hit cyberspace, I got requests for information about the translation rights within two days and was recently offered agent representation by Karen Solem of Writers House.

None of this would have happened if I hadn't taken the chance on a new form of publishing via the Internet for a book that everyone had given up on but me.

Pauline Baird Jones (*www.paulinebjones.com*) is the author of *Do Wah Diddy . . . Die*, aka *I Love Luci—When I Don't Want to Kill Her*, the first e-book sold to Hollywood.

20

TEN TIPS FOR WEAVING YOUR PROMOTIONAL WEB

Karen Wiesner

When I sold my first book to an electronic publisher in 1998, I faced quite a few facts: I didn't know the first thing about the medium, I didn't know how to promote in the medium, and I didn't know if there was even an audience for it. So how do you target an audience you can't identify? I realized that the first step was to educate myself about e-publishing. The next was to educate my fellow authors and the public in order to gain an audience for my books. Success for an e-published author can be achieved only by telling readers, first, what electronic publishing is and, second, why they should read *your* electronic books. Promotion for e-authors is also different and more vital than for traditional authors, and here are ten tips to get you started:

1. Have a personal Web page, somewhere you can send readers to find everything they need to know about you, how to and why to read your books. An e-author without a Web site is like a cat without claws. No way to climb up! Very few e-authors succeed without a Web page.
2. Promote heavily on the Web. Search the Web for places to promote yourself through interviews, live chats, reviews, title listings, and so on. Never let an opportunity pass by to get your name out there. You want to be everywhere readers and writers converge online.
3. Don't neglect off-line promotion, such as attending and speaking at conferences, joining book signings with fellow authors, and putting ads in trade magazines, press releases, and kits. There is no One-Shot-to-the-Stars in any medium and there are no promotional avenues

that are failures. Everything you can do to create a web of intrigue around you and your work is successful. Remember that word of mouth starts with one person telling another person.

4. Establish a presence for yourself in your chosen medium. Make sure the authors know you, publishers know you, and readers know you. Connections often lead to opportunities to promote and move up the success ladder. Gather connections religiously.

5. Be honest. The most effective salesman is the one who tells the truth. To sell a product (or in this case a *medium*), you can't tell all the good things and leave out the bad. E-publishing has disadantages, there are unappealing aspects as well as fantastic, unequaled opportunities. I use the Golden Rule: If I knew nothing about e-publishing, would I prefer someone to tell me, "This is the greatest thing in the world! Nothing bad can happen. Once you sell that book to an e-publisher, you can just lay back and take it easy. You'll make a million." Or would I rather have all the facts set before me—good and bad—and then make my choice? Certainly I and most other authors want to hear all sides of the story. When you use this technique, your audience doesn't leave thinking, "Wow! This sounds too good to be true. Maybe it *is* too good to be true. Maybe I shouldn't even try it." Instead, they leave saying, "Well, there are some downsides, but the potential here, the advantages, are greater than the risks. I know I have some work ahead of me, but I can do it now that I know the lay of the land."

6. Be creative in your promotion. An exciting new medium invites exciting new methods of promotion. Try things that have never been done before, revise those that have been done to match your personality and ability. You never know what will work to increase your exposure.

7. The humble writer is the loser in this competitive game of publishing. Let's face it: Promotion of oneself is a conceited business, but that doesn't make it any less necessary. To be a success, you must look like a success, sound like someone who knows what they're talking about, believe in yourself enough to say "I'm good. I'm worth reading!"

8. Don't limit yourself to one medium. We're entering a wonderful new age in publishing where rights can be unbundled, where authors are free to pursue all of their individual options: print, electronic, audio, and screenplays. Use your rights to expand your résumé and your fan-base.

9. Schedule time to write and time to promote. Authors who write and never promote are disappointed come payday. Authors who promote

but never write don't have a second offering for all the fans they're amassing. Be professional and savvy in your quest for success.

10. Don't neglect your fans. Each and every person who takes the time to sign my guestbook and write to me receives a personal reply. Continue to write outstanding books that transcend genres and mediums. Don't write for the sake of having work out there. Write for love. Care about your fans and their enjoyment as well as your own. Set high standards for yourself. While someday I hope that I'll be so fabulously successful I won't have time for personal responses, I will always honor my fans with a great story.

Karen Wiesner is the bestselling author of *Electronic Publishing: The Definitive Guide (The Most Complete Reference to Non-Subsidy E-Publishing),* as well as three on-going fiction series' and a monthly *Inkspot* column titled "Electronic Publishing Q&A." For more information, visit her Web site at *karenwiesner.hypermart.net.*

21

LIST YOUR BOOK WITH ONLINE BOOKSELLERS—AND YOUR CUSTOMERS WILL FIND YOU

Lauri Ann Randolph

THANK GOD FOR AMAZON.COM!

Over the years, starting in college, I have had many different ideas for cookbooks. Several times I had briefly looked into what it might take to write a cookbook and to get it published. I was always overwhelmed when trying to understand the publishing industry. I concluded that in order to have a book (of any type) published, you needed at least one of the following criteria:

- Be famous already
- Know someone in the publishing industry
- Have a remarkable and/or unique book idea
- Be financially independent and not really care much about the time expended or about the amount of money that would be coming in
- Have enough time and money to do everything yourself (self-publish)

I also found out that getting a book published through traditional means was not necessarily profitable for the author unless it was basically a bestseller, and not every book can do that! When I realized that the author was the last to get paid and received a small percentage after all involved (publisher, distributor, bookstore, agent) took their cuts, I couldn't imagine an ordinary person wanting to write a book of any type, except for the pure love of it. Unless the book hit the bestseller list, how could you make a living at it?

Then one day (months after I had quit corporate America in search of a less stressful lifestyle, but starting to struggle to find a suitable income), my mother sent me a cookbook that her garden club had put together to raise some money for the club. It was published through Cookbooks by Morris Press, which specializes in putting together cookbooks for clubs, churches, and other nonprofit organizations as fund raisers, using recipes from the members of the organization. I called their toll-free number and then received, through the mail, a wonderful package on how to get a cookbook published through them. It was so very, very simple. So I started writing up my recipes using their system.

Months prior to receiving my mother's gift, I was having great success in losing weight on the Dr. Atkin's Diet, which is a low-carbohydrate diet. The diet was easy for me because it had many foods that I loved to eat anyway. But it was restrictive in many ways, too, and I was starting to get bored with it. Realizing I needed more variety in my diet, and after trying to find some low-carb cookbooks with little success, I started making up my own recipes and writing them down, thus beginning *Lauri's Low-Carb Cookbook*.

While the system used by Cookbooks by Morris Press may be quite easy, it was also limiting some things I wanted to do. I made the compromises and had 350 books printed. During the printing time, I started to read books on self-publishing to figure out how I might market the book (other than to friends and family). It was then that I thought I had made a mistake having the books printed. The marketing process looked too difficult. I wondered if I would ever sell enough of the cookbooks even to pay off the printing costs.

I then started surfing the Web looking for Web sites that promote low-carb products that might be willing to set up a system to sell my books for me, but had little success. That's when I found out about Amazon.com and their Advantage Program: "Leveling the playing field for independent books, music, and video." I applied to have Amazon.com carry *Lauri's Low-Carb Cookbook* and sent Amazon.com the simple materials they requested. Within two weeks, my cookbook was accepted, I had a title page on the Amazon.com Web site, and I had my first book order! I then was able to get a variety of low-carb Web sites to link to my Amazon.com title page.

The first month, March 1999, I sold 92 books on Amazon.com! During the second month, the cookbook started selling even better, so I called Morris Press to have 1,100 more books printed. By July, I had sold all the books and was consistently ranked in the top five hundred bestselling books on Amazon. This was simply amazing to me!

In May 1999, I started putting together the second edition of *Lauri's Low-Carb Cookbook*. Since I was not completely satisfied with the compromises I had to make with Morris Press and since I knew that there was a demand for my cookbook, I began to work with a full-service printer directly (Eastwood Printing in Denver, Colorado). I now had complete freedom to put it together the way I really wanted it. I added new recipes, dramatically improved the recipe format, had a much better cover design, improved binding quality, and more. I am very pleased with the process of working with Eastwood Printing and the final product of the second edition. The second edition of the cookbook was listed on Amazon.com, as simply as the first edition, and in only two months I had sold over 750 copies.

Due to the Amazon.com success of *Lauri's Low-Carb Cookbook,* customers are placing special orders at bookstores and sending in the mail order form from the back of the cookbook. With this proven success with the cookbook, Ingram Book Company and Baker & Taylor have recently accepted my book for distribution. There are also some independent bookstores in the Denver area carrying my cookbook on their shelves (due to my personal door-to-door marketing) and soon my cookbook will be carried in many bookstores. Recently, Borders.com and Barnes&Noble.com started carrying my cookbook on their Web sites, too. I think I'm on my way!

Lauri Ann Randolph is the author of *Lauri's Low-Carb Cookbook: Rapid Weight Loss with Satisfying Meals* (2nd Edition ISBN 0-9667963-1-4).

22

START SMALL, BUT THINK BIG

Paulette Ensign

Way back in 1991, when my organizing business was already eight years old, I spotted an offer for a free copy of a booklet called "117 Ideas for Better Business Presentations." Well, because I do business presentations and because the price was right, I sent for it. My first reaction was, "Geez, I could knock something like this out about organizing tips." Then I threw it in a drawer.

Six months later I was sitting in my office, bored, baffled, and beaten down by the difficulty of selling my consulting services and workshops. I had no money and I mean *no money!*

I remembered that little booklet. I had no idea how I was going to do it, but something hit me, and I knew I had to produce a booklet on organizing tips.

I started dumping all those ideas I ever had about getting organized into a file on my computer. These were all pearls that came out of my mouth when I was with clients or when I did a speaking engagement or a seminar. I could do two sixteen-page booklets, each fitting into a number ten envelope, one on business organizing tips and another on household organizing tips. The first one was "110 Ideas for Organizing Your Business Life" and the second one was "111 Ideas for Organizing Your Household."

My first run was 250 copies. That was the most expensive per-unit run I made, but I had to get samples to distribute to start making money.

The only way I could think of selling the booklets was by sending a copy to magazines and newspapers, asking them to use excerpts and putting an invitation at the bottom for readers to send $3 plus a self-addressed, stamped envelope. I had no money to advertise.

Then the orders started dribbling in, envelopes with $3 checks in them or three one-dollar bills. This was great stuff. I remember the day the first one arrived. It was like manna from heaven: $3! Of course, the fact that it took about six months from first starting to write the booklet until the first $3 arrived somehow didn't matter at that moment.

I cast seeds all over the place, hoping that some would sprout. I found directories of publications at the library and started building my list.

Finally, in February 1992, "the big one" hit. A biweekly newsletter with 1.6 million readers ran nine lines of copy about my business booklet. They didn't even use an excerpt! I distinctly remember the day I went to my post office box and found a little yellow slip in my box. It said, "See clerk." There was a *tub* of envelopes that had arrived that day, about 250 as I recall, each with $3 in it. All told, that newsletter mention sold 5,000 copies of my booklet.

In April, that same biweekly newsletter ran a similar nine lines about my household booklet, starting all over again. This time I sold 3,000 copies.

Round about June, I stopped and assessed what had happened. Was I making any money? By then, I had sold about 15,000 copies of the business and the household organizing tips booklets, one copy at a time for $3. When I checked my financial records, I realized I had tediously generated not a ton of money.

And some of the lessons I had learned along the way were expensive ones. I didn't realize my bank was charging me 12¢ for each item deposited until I got my first bank statement with a service charge of $191.

Some very wonderful things happened while selling those 15,000 copies, though.

- A public seminar company ordered a review copy to consider building another product from my booklet. They did, and I recorded an audio program based on the booklet. I sold that tape to my clients as well and it led to a twenty-minute interview on a major airline's in-flight audio program during November and December one year.
- I was sorting through the envelopes . . . $3, $3, $1,000, $3 . . . wait a minute. A manufacturer's rep decided to send my booklets to his customers that year instead of an imprinted calendar!
- A company asked me to write a booklet that was more specific to their product line.

- I got speaking engagements from people who bought the booklet.
- I found out that the list of people who bought my booklet was a salable product.

Things were starting to pick up. So, back to June and taking stock of where I was. You know those advertising card decks in the mail? Well, that day in June I was so bored, I opened one. Glancing through it, I said, "Hey, here's a company that oughta see my booklet. And here's another one, and another one." I sent booklets to each.

Less than a week later, a woman called. At first, it sounded like a prospecting call. Fortunately, I wasn't too abrupt with her. She was calling to ask me the cost of 5,000 customized copies of my booklet for an upcoming trade show. She wanted to know if I could match a certain price.

I slightly underbid her price. She was thrilled and the sale was a done deal. I thought, "Oh, it will be easy to sell large quantities now." Wrong. It was another three or four months until the next large-quantity sale. But, the trade show they were attending was an organization I had contacted about getting my booklet into their catalog. They had rejected it because I wasn't in their industry. But my buyer had bought 5,000 copies of my booklet, with my company information in it, to distribute at that trade show. I loved it!

One day, a guy I know from a major consumer mail-order catalog company said, "Why don't you license us reprint rights to your booklet? We can buy print cheaper than you, so if you charged us a few cents a unit, you wouldn't have to do production." Well, eighteen months later, after lots of zigging and zagging, that sale happened: a non-exclusive agreement for them to print 250,000 copies. We exchanged a ten-page contract for a five-digit check.

They provided the booklet free with any purchase in one issue of their catalog and made a 13 percent increase in sales in that issue. They were happy. I was happy.

I looked for other licensing prospects, even though it had taken eighteen months for this sale to happen, and the five-digit check was low five-digits, not enough to sustain me.

In spring 1993, I designed a class on how to write and market booklets and wrote an eighty-page manual. The class was small and mostly people I knew. They paid me money, and I had a chance to test-run the class. So now, I had another new product, an eighty-page manual, a blueprint of what I had learned about selling my booklet.

I like teaching and now I had a new topic besides the organizing I had been presenting. I also like traveling. So I took the three-hour class on the road and had great fun doing it.

I toured the country for about two years, six to eight classes a year. Many people have written interesting booklets on all kinds of topics. Some have hired me to write a customized marketing plan for their booklet or to coach them by phone to develop their booklet business.

Midway through that year, in August 1994, I discovered CompuServe. My sole purpose for getting online was to market my business. The third day I was online, I saw a forum message from a guy from Italy who had a marketing company there. He told me his client base was small businesses and companies that served small businesses. I told him I had a booklet he might find useful. I sent it to him, he liked it, and we struck a deal. He translated, produced, and marketed it, and agreed to pay me royalties on all sales. He made the first sale of 105,000 copies to a magazine that bundled a copy of my booklet with one issue of their publication. He wired several thousand dollars to my checking account from Italy. All this from someone I had never spoken to and had only communicated with online, by fax, earth mail, and electronic funds transfer. That meant I had sold more than 400,000 copies of my booklet, in two languages, without spending a penny on advertising.

One slow week, I posted a message on some online forums about the story of the Italian booklet as an example of an online success story. Even though blatant selling is not allowed, creating mutually beneficial relation-ships is. Folks who read those postings replied that they would be interested in doing the same thing with my booklet, but in French and Japanese. This had never even dawned on me.

I have had discussions with people in ten different countries. Once these relationships are established, it makes sense to discuss brokering some of the other booklets I have access to among the people from my classes or those whom I've coached or who have bought my manual.

I've also discovered licensing opportunities for my booklet content in other formats.

- Two different companies that produce laminated guides (one hinged, the other spiral bound) licensed my content.
- My organizing company was replaced by my company Tips Products International.

- I've started writing tips for booklet production and other uses by recycling the client's existing materials into tips.
- I've been writing customized marketing plans for people's booklets for a while now.
- The latest addition is the creation of an e-booklet catalog on my Web site where other people's booklets are sold as downloadable e-booklets.

I never could have written a business plan for how this has all unfolded.

Paulette Ensign is the Founder, CEO, and Chief Visionary of the San Diego–based Tips Products International. For information about ways you can duplicate and surpass her own successes, visit her Web site at www.tipsbooklets.com.

ACCESSING NEWSGROUPS, LISTSERVS, WEB SITES, AND ONLINE BOOKSTORES

James A. Cox

Being able to publicize and promote books effectively on the Internet is a vital marketing skill for small, midsized, and specialty publishers in today's fiercely competitive marketplace. Selling books on the Internet is not a luxury for a bit more cash flow, it's a necessity for sheer financial survival.

Here are some tips, tricks, and techniques for identifying and accessing Internet newsgroups (online discussion groups), listservs, Web sites, and online bookstores that will enable the independent publisher to succeed in this new and growing medium.

- Assess your book in terms of key descriptive words. Write them all down.
- Assess your book's author in terms of background, experience, associations, credentials, education, and previously published works (articles, essays, books, and so on). Write all these key words down as well.
- If you have America Online (AOL), go to the AOL home page and type the word "newsgroups" into the search feature. This will take you to AOL's newsgroup identification and sign-up feature. Just follow the onscreen instructions. They are simple and straightforward. Identify all the newsgroups that are thematically linked to the key words related to your book and its author.

  For all other Internet service provider accounts, go to Deja.com at *www.deja.com/usenet/*. On the home page of this search engine for newsgroups and listservs, you will find a Quick Search function. Type your key words into it (one word per search) and locate those Internet discussion groups that are thematically appropriate to your book and/or author.

- Go to the *Midwest Book Review* Web site at *www.execpc.com/~mbr/ bookwatch/writepub*. There you will find a section devoted to search engines. Go down them (you might want to start with Google.com, it's my personal favorite) entering in your key words to locate thematically appropriate Internet discussion groups and Web sites.

- Go to the *Midwest Book Review* Web site section *www.execpc.com/ ~mbr/bookwatch/booklove*. There you will find a huge section of online bookstore links. It contains links to hundreds of specific bookstores, as well as to Web sites that have bookstore databases of hundreds more. Bookmark this page for future use.

- Once you have located a thematically appropriate discussion group, Web site, or online bookstore, either bookmark them or just copy and paste their URLs onto a "future contact" list.

   Note: All publishers, regardless of the nature of their book, should include *alt.books.review* because that is a generic or generalist book-oriented newsgroup of librarians, bookstore retailers, and the general reading public that has about ninety thousand subscribers worldwide.

- Sign up with all thematically appropriate newsgroups and listservs. Download them for a few days to read their communication traffic and get a feel for the kind of discussions that go on.

   Explore the bookstore Web pages to determine if they are a general store or a specialty dealer. All general online bookstores are feasible for future promotional contacts. Specialty stores should only be contacted if your book fits within their area of focus.

- Prepare four different types of publicity material (more on what goes into press releases and articles a bit later):

   1. The short press release e-mail: a hundred words or less
   2. The medium press release e-mail: 100 to 300 words
   3. The long press release e-mail: over 300 words
   4. An article based on or drawn from your book

You will want to register your individual Web page with some of the search engines. Some of them want the short description, others the medium, still others allow unlimited (long) descriptions. This is all material that can be easily drawn from your press release write-ups.

- Send the appropriate publicity release in the form of an e-mail to all the targeted bookstores.
- Contact thematically appropriate Web site owners with an offer to exchange links.
- Framing the press release e-mail:

    Take the same information that is to be found in any competent paper format press release (see Chapter 32) and rewrite it within the body of an e-mail document. Never, ever, attach a press release to an e-mail document—ever! Put all of your information into the body of the e-mail, cast in the form of a letter to the recipient as follows:

DEAR XXX:

THE DESCRIPTIVE CONTENT OF YOUR BOOK HERE.

THE CITATION OF YOUR AUTHOR'S CREDENTIALS AND BACKGROUND HERE.

THE ORDERING OR CONTACT INFORMATION HERE.

YOUR SIGNATURE AND WEB SITE URL HERE.

The key to an effective e-mail press release is the "soft sell," a brief (one paragraph) description followed by a sentence on why it should be of interest to the subscribers of that particular newsgroup or listserv, or the owner of that particular Web site, or that the potential readership is of a size to be profitable to that particular online bookstore. In other words, what's in it for them (entertainment, information, profit)? Gear the payoff to the recipient.

- The Article: Prepare an article on the subject matter of your book. Pretend that you've just been invited by a major magazine to write a couple hundred words on the subject and given permission to cite your book as a reference for further study on the matters covered. For most newsgroups, all listservs, and specialized Web sites you will be using the article, and not the press release e-mail to promote and publicize your book. For online bookstores, you will primarily use the press release statement, followed up by the article. One of the things to note is whether or not booksellers' sites allow visitors to post comments or reviews of books already in their inventories (Amazon.com does, as do a few of the others). When you see this opportunity, post all the positive reviews you have received from other sources (*Midwest Book Review, Publishers Weekly, Library Journal,* local newspapers, etc.).

If you don't see this "posting" feature on the Web site, then send positive reviews (as they come in to you from reviewers) to the bookstores as simple e-mail messages.

- Once you've established yourself with an Internet discussion group and have led off with your article, you can then post (not all at once, but spaced out over time, no more often than once a week) those "review" e-mails that you've prepared for use with the bookstores. This keeps your title visible by noting those new reviewers and their publications as the sources. Preface each of these posts with something like "Another great review just came in and I thought I'd pass it along. You can find more information on our Web site at . . ."

- Currently, every review generated by the *Midwest Book Review* is posted to the following:

  Amazon.com
  ReadersNdex
  Books.com
  BookWire
  alt.books.review
  Review Index (a Gale Research Company interactive CD-ROM)

  Additionally, we also post thematically appropriate reviews to the following newsgroups:

  alt.animals
  alt.architecture
  alt.art
  alt.books.technical (computer books & software reviews)
  alt.buddha
  alt.business
  alt.cooking-chat
  alt.cooking-cook
  alt.cooking-cooking
  alt.folklore
  alt.history
  alt.literacy.adult

alt.metaphysics.lightwork
alt.old-west
alt.railroads
rec.arts.mystery
rec.arts.sf.written

The *Midwest Book Review* also posts its reviews on:

Internet Bookwatch e-mail subscription list
Children's Bookwatch e-mail subscription list

Particular review columns (cookbooks, parenting, theater/cinema, money/finance, metaphysics, etc.) are then sent via e-mail to their own list of subscribers, folks who didn't want to wade through an entire Internet Bookwatch issue to get the reviews in their particular areas of interest. Several of these folks use the reviews (giving credit to *Midwest Book Review* as the source) to bolster the informational content of their own Web sites.

By the way, you will also find a list of links to online magazines on our Web site at *www.execpc.com/~mbr/bookwatch/booklove*. Consider any of these for submitting that article drawn from your book for publication. It's just another way to get a bit of promotion on the Internet.

· Once you have joined a newsgroup or listserv, you don't have to download their messages automatically or forever. You can simply set them to store up and then, after a period of time, either delete them or scan them for headings that you might want to respond to.

To summarize, the technique for successful e-mail marketing posts is:

1. Keep your message short, simple and complete
2. Identify the value of the message for the recipient
3. Send the message to newsgroups, listservs, etc., that are thematically appropriate

And remember that Internet marketing has a lot in common with door-to-door selling. You may need to make a hundred contacts to get a single sale. Some folks will object to being interrupted by you. Others may be too busy to respond. But the virtue of the computer is that you can knock on those cyberspace doors with just the touch of a keyboard button, and without the overhead costs of gas for the car, stamps for the envelopes, or dogs going for your pant cuff.

———————————————

James A. Cox is Editor-in-Chief of the *Midwest Book Review* (*www.execpc.com/~mbr/bookwatch*).

24

WORKING THE NET: ORGANIZATION AND TIME MANAGEMENT

Jamie Engle

From the moment I signed on to AOL and wandered into one of the communities, the possibilities of mixing the Net with marketing and promotion boggled my mind. That same expansiveness can break your Net marketing and PR efforts, however. Learning how to manage information influx is the key to successful PR, and to keeping current with your chosen industry. Organization and time management keep information fresh and accessible.

Planning is the key to organization and time management. E-books have a longer shelflife, giving you more time to promote your title. It takes planning to keep your promotion campaign going that long. You have to be ready to follow up on the new-release splash. Planning which marketing and PR tools to use tightens the scope of your focus and the amount of information you need to gather.

Poring over every digest, newsletter, e-zine, or site update for the "gems," it's easy to get bogged down in e-mail. If you open the e-mail, file it where relevant and archive it separately. Remember to keep source and copyright information intact. It's helpful to keep a paper list of file names and content, otherwise you could end up with three files with the same information. If there's a deadline for action, mark it down on your calendar. Make it a habit to mark and, most important, read your calendar regularly.

Following leads on new sites or publications usually means surfing the Net. Following link lists while doing research can be a sure time-burner, but sometimes turns up a nugget or two. Remember to keep focused and targeted. Leave a certain amount of time for wandering, but know when to stop and come back later—and don't forget to go back to it. Use folders to organize your bookmarks and mark one "Sites to Follow Up On." The super-organized will have a follow-up folder for each topic, making it even easier to find sites related to current research needs. It's also a good idea to sign up for the site's newsletter or page change notification service. Besides reminding you to go back to the site, the newsletter gives you an idea of the site's style and format.

Have a plan of attack for reading the site. Know what information you need so you can gather it all at one time. If the information isn't on site, e-mail for it. Make a note of when the information was requested, and follow up if necessary. I find it helpful to record basic information on an index card, with simple cross-references. It takes a little bit of time, but in the event of a computer crash, can save you from starting at ground zero.

Maximizing your resources is another way to manage your time. Look for sites that provide content to other sites, and send your review submissions, news releases, and announcements there. Let them send it to other sites for you. If not used, then you can send to the other sites individually. A real gem provides content to both print publications and Web sites, and probably has stricter submission guidelines. Following submission guidelines improves the chances of your piece being used.

Using these few commonsense guidelines, you will get more from your Net marketing and promotion efforts, and it will pay off in the best ways possible: more resources, contacts, time, and sales.

Jamie Engle is owner of the e-book Connections Web site (*www.ebookconnections.com*), an information portal for the e-publishing and e-book communities, including e-book reviews. eBC's site content, reviews, and e-newsletter are distributed industry-wide. Jamie's articles also appear in publishing, writer, and reader magazines and e-zines.

25

HOW TO BE *EVERYWHERE* ON THE INTERNET: CREATING A CREDIBLE ONLINE REPUTATION

Cathy Stucker

Lots of people believe that success in business is all about who you know. But even more important than who you know is who knows you.

Think of it this way: You belong to many communities—your city or town, your family, your industry, the company you work for, the clubs and organizations to which you belong, and so on. One of the ways you grow a business or promote yourself is through connections you make in your communities. People do business with you because they know and trust you.

There are many communities within the online world as well. The Internet is not just a lot of nameless, faceless, anonymous digital bits and bytes. It is people relating to other people. It is also people buying from other people. In order to attract business and become successful through the Internet, you need to create an online reputation. This means you must become known and establish your credibility in targeted online communities.

Just as in offline marketing, it is important to get in front of people often. It's not enough for someone to see your name one place, or read one article by or about you. They need to have the feeling that they see you everywhere they go.

How can you be *everywhere* on the Internet? It's easier than it seems. You don't literally have to be everywhere. You just want the people you want to attract to see you in several places. When your name keeps popping up, they'll think they have seen you everywhere, and they will look at you as an important figure in your field.

Where will your potential customers go when they are online? By answering a few simple questions, you'll know, and you'll know how you can be there, too.

What Web sites do they already visit? Go to those sites and see how you might be able to make your presence felt there. Could you supply articles or other content? Would the site owner create a link to your site? Are there discussion boards where you can post messages? Does the site include resource information, and should you be listed as a resource? Do they review products? Can you advertise on the site?

What e-mail lists and discussion groups will your customers be in? Subscribe and participate.

What e-zines do they subscribe to (and actually read)? Offer articles or consider placing an ad. One of the most successful methods for me has been writing articles that have been picked up by e-zines, print newsletters, and magazines. You can open a free account and make your articles available at Idea Marketers (*www.ideamarketers.com*).

What terms will your customers enter in search engines? Make sure you include them in your Web site's meta tags and on your main page.

Where will they look for experts in your field? Are there organizations you should belong to or directories where you should be listed? I recently received a prominent mention on the CNN-fn Web site because the reporter found me listed at the Association of Authors and Publishers site (*www.authorsandpublishers.org*).

Who are the leaders and opinion-shapers in your field? Make yourself known to them. Many people, even famous and powerful people, are accessible by e-mail. Can you introduce yourself or offer them something they might be interested in?

As you look for ways to be visible, imagine that customers are looking for information on your topic. They do an online search and find several Web sites, including yours. When they start to visit the other sites, they run across reviews of your product, interviews with you, articles by you, links to your site, and so on. They join a mailing list and see your posts and people talking about you. It seems that everywhere they look, they find you. To them, you are *everywhere* on the Internet. Doing business with you is almost inevitable at that point.

Don't rely solely on online methods to get attention, though. One way I get subscribers to my online e-zines is very low tech. When I present a seminar, I invite the participants to subscribe simply by checking a box on the class roster.

Get publicity in online and offline media by sending press releases to announce your news. Hold events such as online chats, teleclasses, and book signings. Come up with an unusual angle to interest the media. Could you hold an online book signing for your new e-book? How would it work?

Declare your own holiday and promote it. I have created several holidays, including Someday, the day to do all those things you've been putting off until "someday." (By the way, it's September 15th.) All you need to do to declare your holiday is decide when it is and what it is called, then announce it through press releases and by notifying companies that produce lists of such holidays. You can list your holiday at Chase's Calendar of Events *(www.chases.com)* and Celebrate Today! *(www.celebratetoday.com)*. My holidays have been featured in books and magazines, I've been interviewed on the radio all over the country, and Someday has been included in some of the planners produced by Franklin Covey.

Create alliances with those businesses that complement yours. If you are trying to reach the same market but are not in direct competition, you can help each other.

Give away samples. I have given non-exclusive rights to articles and special reports to publishers who include them in e-books, books, and manuals that they sell. I don't profit directly from this, but it increases awareness of me, and demonstrates my expertise to a new audience.

Use these techniques and more to get in front of your target market repeatedly, demonstrate your expertise, and build a credible reputation. Be creative and have fun coming up with new ways to get attention. The more you do, the more success will come your way.

Visit Cathy Stucker on the web at *www.idealady.com* for more information on ways to get online publicity, and to subscribe to her free e-zines. Or send a blank e-mail to *moreinfo@idealady.com*.

26

BLURBS SELL BOOKS

Sally J. Walker

I believe the "Gotcha Chain" of bookselling includes title, cover, author name–recognition, and blurbs, those pithy paragraphs on the back of print books, the short summaries that copywriters at big publishing houses provide for their catalogs, or what e-publishers put on each book's Web page. In fact, for some e-publishers, that singular little paragraph is the only information provided to help readers make their buying decision.

The first three links in the chain all have potential weaknesses: Titles cannot be copyrighted, but must be appropriate to the book and, above all, memorable. Since beauty is in the eye of the beholder, not everyone agrees on tasteful, genre-appropriate, or even memorable covers. And authors have to work for years (at least two or three) to develop a loyal readership that clamors for the next book. So where do blurbs enter the equation?

In my estimation blurbs are the unrecognized, undervalued diamonds in the Gotcha Chain. As daily life becomes more hectic, the marketing value of blurbs will increase proportionately.

That one paragraph can make the sale or cause the rejection. Why? Time and intrigue. The busy consumer will spend seconds reading a blurb rather than minutes skimming a sample of the book. If the blurb intrigues the reader to want more, the skimming of a posted sample may come next. If the blurb sounds like many others of that genre or another rehash of a tired storyline, the reader can zip on to another blurb, another book. The title, the cover, the author may all entice the reader to hesitate, but the consumer decides to stay or move on according to how interesting they find the blurb.

In the world of print marketing, everyone knows that the book distributors and chain buyers don't read entire books before choosing them for warehousing and distribution and giving them shelf space. With the volume of printed matter, these harried people must rely on what? The blurbs in the catalog coming from each publisher.

Perhaps a marketing blitz here and there will focus attention on a particular book or line of books. Most of the time, however, if the distributor or buyer has no personal preference, those pithy paragraphs will be the only exposure they have to a book. When a consumer is surfing the Net for a new read, they are in the same position. The blurb determines the selection of that book.

For over five years I have belonged to a readers' group that meets monthly to peruse all the publishers' catalogs. The group was founded by an independent bookseller who makes the publications available to us, along with substantial discounts on our orders. The attendees are of varied social, economic, and educational background. One thing we have in common is the love of an enthralling story. Book covers have very little significance to us.

First, we ask about books coming out by favorite authors. Then we move on to titles. If a title catches someone's attention, the blurb is read aloud. By blurb alone we decide whether to order or pass.

Some paragraphs sadly could be cut and pasted right onto another book's space. Maybe that one was read last year or five years ago or, even sadder, just last month. An example might be:

The rakehell earl relieved his boredom by becoming the infamous High Road Highwayman. The only passenger in this coach turns out to be his new ward, a beautiful, virginal urchin with fire in her soul and an inheritance he desperately needs.

Others are so vague that no one buys, even if the author is a favorite. The attitude is "If the marketing people couldn't be interested enough in the story to be more specific, then why should we buy it?" An invented example of this type:

How can the starship commander tolerate one last voyage with his loyal crew? And yet the mission must be attempted or the galaxy is lost.

Each blurb for fiction must deliver the taste of an intriguing story, dynamic character, and an aching problem, all so unique that the consumer *has* to buy that book.

When so much information is available on the Internet, the electronic publisher also needs pithy paragraphs that will catch the reader's interest.

They must be short, genuinely dramatic, and unique. The writer who can provide that paragraph is a valuable asset.

EVOLUTION OF SUMMARIZING

Historically, the creative writer's imagination birthed a story. That person then slaved over blank page after blank page to produce the first draft. Most artists then reread their masterpiece, decided it was garbage, and revised it until a polished diamond emerged from the coal. The final step was to send off the four hundred pages to a publisher who would hopefully pore over the entire manuscript and send back rave comments and a hefty check. Historically this may have been the process. No more.

Today, anyone marketing stories must know how to summarize, because the people on the receiving end do not have time to pore over anything. Summarizing is an art form all by itself and it is an incredibly painful art form. The creative birthing, the actual writing and revising are obviously still part of the process, but our "Age of Hurry" often dictates that the 90,000-word book be condensed to various lengths for marketing purposes. Rare is the agent, editor, or distributor who is going to read an entire book to determine its value. I'll say it again: Busy people don't have that kind of time. And the closer the book gets to the consumer, the shorter the condensed version.

Writers' guides often say works of fiction should be submitted to publishers with the first three chapters (to see if the writer can write) and a synopsis (to see if the writer can tell a good, unique story appropriate to the needs of the publisher). Most synopses are one to four pages long or 250 to 1,000 words and must deliver the unique flavor of the characters, their motivations, and the highlights of the story's journey. This is where the writer is allowed to tell, not show. The busy person does not want to be dazzled with details. Synopsis is the bare bones of story and character. At the far end of the summation spectrum is what is called the "log line." In the film industry this is the one-liner that appears in *TV Guide* or on the

Preview Channel. The story and focal characters are described in fewer than twenty-five words.

In the book industry, both writers and editors need log lines because this is the simplest reply to "What's the book about?" The memorized sentence is recited.

Think of the log line as the touted "hook." When the consumer is surfing the TV channels or the Net, one-liners make them pause. If query letters to publishing houses deliver that hook up-front in the opening paragraph, the writer is demonstrating 1) the powerful focus of the book's essence and 2) that incredibly valuable ability to summarize. Hook their attention in very few words and then draw them into that blurb paragraph where the fish want to climb into your boat and take that fantasy voyage, spending hours reading that story. A good blurb will result in the editor requesting the synopsis and three chapters . . . or the reader buying the book to read all 90,000 words.

ELEMENTS OF A BLURB

When writers are learning to do face-to-face pitches to editors, trial and error teaches they do not have the time to explain the nuances of plot, subplot, back story, and character angst. If the writer starts to ramble trying to get all this in, the editor grows bored and, sometimes, annoyed.

So, the wise writer learns to condense the interesting elements of their book into a concise description of a unique beginning-middle-ending story, with appealing, believable characters. These are the simple elements the editor needs to decide if the book fits that publisher's readership, and if time should be spent evaluating the standard synopsis and first three chapters.

In other words, what makes this story different, memorable, worthy of publishing, worthy of purchasing, worthy of time out of a reader's life . . . in one hundred words or less?

EXAMPLES FROM THE FICTION WORKS

Charlie Vogel is a retired Omaha police officer who is turning out superb and unusual mysteries for The Fiction Works. Here is the blurb for *To Find a Killer:*

Bob Norris witnessed his wealthy wife's murder in a convenience store and knew it wasn't coincidental to the robbery. Leaving his job as an art teacher, he moves into the seamy slums of Pecatonica, Nebraska, to team up with a gusty one-armed man and a slick little streetwalker. His amateur sleuthing turns him into a dangerous man willing to do anything to find the killer and the man who hired him. [71 words]

The reader is given specifics about the unique story, the not-so-common characters, and the purposes that drives them to a conclusion. Beginning (murder in convenience store), middle (leaves job, joins unusual folk, moves to slums, sleuths), ending (finds the killer and the man who hired him). Only the protagonist, the point-of-view character, is named, with descriptive tags characterizing the other important figures in the story. The reader is left to infer a lot and to ask questions. If the questions are powerful enough, the reader is motivated to buy the book.

When blurbs are used for varied story collections, they resemble the Hollywood log lines, such as the paragraph telling about S. Joan Popek's collection, *The Administrator:*

You will also find answers: a delightful fantasy voyage that puts a new twist on Alzheimer's disease; a drunk, down about as far as she can go, is ready to give up until she meets a different kind of alien, right there in the gutter; a robot suffers from comical depression and a bad case of religion; because of a long-dead prehistoric woman, two space-faring, aging scientists give up their chance for fame and save a world; another world regains life due to one woman's faith; and a not-quite-virgin meets a dragon with a sensitive stomach. [100 words]

My own mainstream collection, *Letting Go of Sacred Things,* has a simpler blurb because it deals with life-stage episodes from the experiences of one woman:

Shy, unassuming Opal grows ever stronger through trial, love, and loss experienced between 1910 and 1981. This poignant saga depicts family dynamics and ten life-stages in the twentieth century's era of changing values. Opal demonstrates that life's knocks teach us to let go of material things and cherish our own spirit and our loved ones.

If greatness lies in survival of each challenge with personal integrity intact, this woman is indeed great. [72 words]

Again, the reader is given the mainstream appeal of complex issues versus simple ones. A forward-moving plotline is implied while offering the intrigue of examining life stages and a century's changing values. The reader finds the essential outline, underlying problem, and a positive outcome, all through the description of a unique character.

IMPORTANCE OF TIME/LENGTH

Okay, so you noticed the word lengths at the end of each example. The majority of those succint paragraphs in print house catalogs are sixty-five to seventy-five words long. Of course, some readers (and writers) may want more, but the questions you have to ask yourself are: How can I tell the most about my story and characters with the least number of words? and Will this paragraph demand that the book be read to answer the questions raised?

Sally J. Walker has been a professional writer for fifteen years. Her credits can be viewed at *www.lbcoyote.com/Bio/Sally/works.htm*. After contracting a second audio book and several novels with The Fiction Works (*www.fictionworks.com*), she now works for the company as editorial director.

Part Three

POUNDING THE VIRTUAL PAVEMENT: SELLING YOUR BOOK ONLINE

27

SELL YOURSELF ON THE NET WITHOUT BREAKING THE BANK

Mary Westheimer

THE NET'S "SECRET WEAPON": THE SIGNATURE

Nearly everyone has a Web site these days, but only one in five even knows about one of the Net's most powerful marketing devices, the lowly "signature."

An e-mail signature is a small text blurb that automatically attaches to the end of your e-mail and newsgroup postings, allowing you to add information about your company, services, and products. This addendum helps spread the word about your offerings without actually selling. You can mention a special sale, promote a client, or boast about your benefits, even if your message itself doesn't even mention your business.

You can tout your company's services in your signature, and have different signatures for different audiences (one for friends, one for customers, and another for vendors, for instance). Does it work? Promoting our publishers in a signature campaign caused sales to increase by as much as 75 percent.

Keep your signature small—a rule of thumb is that a signature shouldn't exceed six lines—and focused on benefits and urgency in the brief description. Also, always use the full URL, including the http://. That makes the address "hot" in most e-mail programs, letting curious readers automatically click through to see the site.

EXTRA! EXTRA! PROFIT FROM THIS NEWS!

Most people know about promoting a Web site through search engines and reciprocal links, but a recent study suggests that newsgroups and mailing lists are one of the most effective ways to drive people to your Web site. BookZone, which has provided Internet hosting, development, and promotion services to more than 3,300 publishing professionals since 1994, asked nearly 9,000 publishers what is working for them online. The survey revealed that those who are most happy with their site traffic are using newsgroups and mailing lists to get the word out. Interestingly enough, fewer survey participants were using newsgroups and mailing lists than search engines, online advertising, linking campaigns, or even strategic alliances.

Newsgroups are online clubs that are not on the Web, but actually reside on another part of the Internet known as the Usenet. To find newsgroups where your audience congregates, visit *www.deja.com*. Their tracker service will even e-mail you with updates on specific subjects. For mailing lists, visit Liszt at *www.liszt.com*.

LOW-COST, HIGH-IMPACT ADVERTISING

Mention "online advertising" and most people immediately think of ad banners. Well, it looks like it's time to think again. Online newsletters, or e-zines, provide the best bang for the buck. E-zine advertising usually costs less, and it reaches a targeted, receptive audience—right in their e-mail in-boxes.

According to Forrester Research, 70 percent of business owners consider this low-cost, highly targeted contact tool an important part of their online marketing strategy. Why? The Forrester study found that e-mail click-through rates—which measure how many people click on a Web site address included in the e-mail—range from 14 to 22 percent, compared to a click-through rate of just 1 percent for graphic banner ads. This makes sense because people who sign up for an e-zine are interested in the subject and are more likely to read it when it arrives.

You can advertise on others' e-zines or start your own. To find out who is already doing what, e-mail Gary Christensen at *Writers98@aol.com* for his "List of 25 Web Locations Where You Can Register Your E-Zine, Free."

SITES OF SUBSTANCE SERVE PUBLISHERS

Of all the things that have changed on the Web since its arrival in 1993, one fact has remained constant: "Content is king." Why are sites always looking for solid information? A Forrester Research survey of 8,600 U.S. households revealed that 75 percent of users said they returned to a site because of good content.

So if you have the "goods," contribute articles or book excerpts (with strong links to your Web site at the bottom) to sites your audience visits. This gives you the editorial impact of public relations and this is a great example of using what we know works offline. Take advantage of the Web's capability for immediate gratification. For more information on content linking, contact BookZone (*www.bookzone.com*).

Mary Westheimer is the CEO of BookZone (*www.bookzone.com*), which has served more than 3,300 publishing professionals with Web hosting, development, and promotion. For more information, visit *www.bookzone.com* or call 800-536-6162.

28

MARKETING 101: WHO IS YOUR AUDIENCE AND WHY THAT MATTERS

M. J. Rose

The very first thing you have to do is figure out who your audience is and then you can begin to work on how to reach them. And the first step in determining your target audience is figuring out your USP.

WHAT IS A USP?

It's advertising lingo. USP stands for a unique selling proposition—a one-liner that defines the unique entity that is your book. Not a two-liner. Not a paragraph. Not a clever advertising slogan. And not a summary of the plot. But rather a one-liner that sets your book apart from all the other books out there. It can be simple. It does not have to be creative. Most of all it has to be to the point.

For my novel, *Lip Service,* I chose, "An erotic and intelligent novel for a woman who thinks."

Why? Because the combination of those two words—erotic and intelligent—was what made my book different. There is a lot of erotica out there, and a lot of smart books out there, but my novel offered a combination of those two things, and few other novels being published at the time offered that distinct combination.

No matter what your novel is about, be it romance, sci-fi, or mystery—I guarantee there is something you can say that defines it.

The reason you need your USP is to figure out exactly who your target audience is. For this book, the USP would be, "What every author needs to know about publishing and promoting online." Don't worry about coming up with a USP that seems to limit your readership. You are going to start out small on purpose.

If you think about the advertising you see on TV, you realize that the same ad that runs on the Super Bowl doesn't run on the Lifetime network—at least not often. That's because the Super Bowl's demographics are different from those of the Lifetime network. Even with those demographic breakdowns, the problem with TV advertising is that there is still an enormous amount of waste. You can only reach your broad general audience.

That's the beauty of the Web. You can narrow your audience down so that you're reaching exactly whom you want to reach.

Say your book is about a powerful female vampire. On TV or in a magazine, you might reach some women who are into sci-fi and women's empowerment issues, but your message will be wasted on the millions of people who are interested in neither. But on the Web you can find dozens of sites, listservs, chat groups, message boards, and newsgroups that talk only to feminists, sci-fi fans, and vampire lovers.

So before you figure out how to get to your target audience, you have to define that audience. Even if you think "everyone who reads" is your target audience, you can't reach everyone who reads. Not even narrowing it down to "every woman who reads" will help much.

You need to find a small subgroup that you can reach without having to spend any money on advertising or public relations—especially if you are like me and you've spent all your extra cash on having the book copyedited.

So my target audience was smart women who liked to read provocative books and women who felt comfortable with their own sexuality. I figured I could find them online and make them aware of my book and that, if I did, they would buy it.

Think about whom your book will appeal to. Don't just say women who read novels. Be much more specific. Women who are breastfeeding their babies . . . men who live in rentals in big cities . . . people who grew up on farms. Because for every niche you can think of, you can find at least one newsgroup, e-zine, newsletter, or listserv on the Web targeted to that group. And as an author, you can use all these outlets to market your novel.

I knew there was an audience for my book because I had been the chief copywriter for Harlequin Books. As part of my job, I attended focus groups, and over a two-year period I met with thousands of women to discuss their reading habits. These groups usually included twelve to eighteen women, married, single, and divorced, from twenty to fifty years old, both working and not. These women fell into two groups: those who read romance novels and those who read commercial or literary fiction.

I heard these women talk about how they used the fantasies they read in books to supplement and enhance their sex lives. I knew that women who were sexually comfortable with themselves were my target audience. Now I just needed to find out where they congregated online.

29

PEOPLE WON'T READ YOUR BOOK IF YOU DON'T MARKET IT

M. J. Rose

Even though my book was in the online bookstores, there were no sales. No one knew it was there! I had submitted my Web site to all the big search engines, but I wasn't getting any traffic. Obviously, until people knew my book existed, no one would go searching for it.

Finding the right environment for your message takes time, but it's worth it. And once you have your USP—that unique selling proposition—you've done the hardest job.

Pick a big search engine. Sherlock if you're on a Mac, Google.com or Dogpile.com if you're on a PC (or Mac). Type in key words that your book's audience might use to search for a book like yours.

Since my USP was "an erotic and intelligent book for a woman who thinks," I looked for erotic, intelligent, and female-friendly Web sites, e-zines, and listservs.

So I typed my keywords—women, erotica, and literature—into the search engines and went to work.

Go to all the sites that come up in the top matches. I went to over eight hundred sites. I followed links and followed those links to other links. I made a list of every site where I thought smart women spent time. I compiled a list of these sites—two hundred of them.

I chose the sites that fit the feel of my book. Not X-rated sites. Not porn sites. Rather, I chose female-friendly, comfortable, intelligent sites that felt good to me. Sites where I'd be proud to have my book discussed.

Making lists and copying the live links to those sites was critical because you can get lost online as you chase sites and get deeper and deeper into the long lists of other sites that might be relevant.

WHAT TO DO WITH SELECTED SITES ONCE YOU HAVE THEM

The next step is to write to every one of those different sites, asking them to either review your book or mention it in some pertinent way.

I wrote three different letters—emphasizing different points and trying different language—then picked fifteen of the smallest sites (ones I didn't really mind losing if my letter bombed) and tested my letter.

I sent five sites my first letter, five sites my second letter, and five sites my third letter. The point of this exercise was to see which letter would generate the most responses—which one communicated best.

When I tabulated the results there was one clear winner. One letter had gotten five responses. One letter had gotten two. And one letter had indeed bombed. Which one had won? The letter that won had included three reader reviews of my novel.

So I can save you a bit of time here. Before you approach anyone, get some reviews of the book.

Not sure of how to get reviews? Find a listserv that discusses books in your genre and offer a free copy of your book to anyone who will review it—if, of course, they like it. Don't ask for favors. You won't have to. There will be people who will want to take you up on your offer. Remember you don't need dozens of reviews to start with, just two or three.

Okay. You've got your USP, your audience, and your reviews. Now what?

Write a letter to the content manager of those perfect sites you found and offer a review copy. If the site didn't seem like the kind of site to review a book, offer to write a five-hundred-word article, *free,* on a subject that fits the site in exchange for their giving you a live link to where readers can buy your novel. The results of all this work can be amazing.

In a matter of three months, my novel was mentioned on over fifty sites and I started getting readers. One of those sites still has one of my free articles up and that article still sends around eighty visitors to my site each month.

GET YOUR BOOK HEARD

On the principle of authors' bookstore readings, there are two Web sites that get serious traffic where you can post audio clips of you reading from your own books.

The benefit of these sites is that they have large audiences of readers who are specifically looking for good books. We've found that listening online is even more entertaining than reading online.

MP3 Lit (*www.mp3lit.com*) works very much on the same principle as its musical counterpart MP3.com. Spend some time on MP3 Lit and listen to some of the interviews and author readings.

If you are a publisher or a published author, contact the submissions editor by e-mail at *submit@mp3lit.com*. There is no charge to have your audio files featured on MP3 Lit, but submissions are subject to their editorial acceptance.

If you are an unpublished or self-published author, go to their Loudmouth section (*www.mp3lit.com/loudmouth/index.html*) and follow the instructions on how to submit your work for free.

Another site, WritersReading (*www.WritersReading.com*) was designed by the creator of The Book Report (*www.bookreport.com*) to encourage readers to discover new authors and new books via audio clips that can be listened to by anyone online.

The benefit of this site is that the audio clips are displayed in banner type ads on the home page of The Book Report site, which gets over 600,000 reader visits a month. Having an audience of over half a million readers a month exposed to your name, the title of your book, and the chance to hear you read from a chapter is very good exposure indeed.

There is a fee at WritersReading, but every author's clip will be highlighted and displayed several times a month via banner type announcements and will be archived by category in a permanent area of the site.

30

BRAINSTORMING TO DEVELOP A MARKETING STRATEGY

M. J. Rose

For several months I held brainstorming chats online at iUniverse.com. The idea was to help writers develop promotional marketing strategies for their books.

Kelly Milner Hall, a talented journalist, acted as host and moderator and invited the authors to join in. In one hour we were always able to come up with several very unusual ways for each writer to promote his or her title.

To help illustrate the process we went through so you can use it yourself, I thought it would be interesting to reprint excerpts from two of those sessions here.

Basically the idea is to focus outside the plot of the book and look for the hooks that you, as the author or publisher, can utilize with the press and the reading public. Think outside the box—look for the unusual—the idea that hasn't been done before—or give an old idea a twist and do it in a new way.

(If you would be interested in participating in sessions like this, e-mail me at *mjRoseAuthor@aol.com* and I'll let you know where and when we will be doing them again.) Here are some highlights from the logs of those sessions:

1: *THE COMPLETE MALE HANDBOOK FOR SEX, DATING AND OTHER TRIVIAL STUFF*, BY PETER BARTULA

M. J. ROSE: Okay . . . so the very first thing we have to do is figure out a great way to get you seen and noticed. We need to start by defining your target audience. Who is the book for, Peter? And don't just say men. Make it specific.

PETER B.: Everyone, even though it sounds like a male 18–30 book, if you aren't a priest or nun, you can learn from this book!

M. J. ROSE: Right, but we need to make it more specific. We can't reach everyone. We have to target.

PETER B.: How about women 18–30. Men are afraid to buy books about this topic.

M. J. ROSE: Okay. So the first thing we do if we are going after women is come up with a hook, and by that I mean something to get you and the book attention. Let's start with some zany ideas.

What if we come up with a holiday—The Date Day, May 16th? And what we do is announce all over the place that May 16th is Date Day, and we run contests for the best dates you've ever been on. Get one of the online greeting card companies to add Date Day. Peter, write op-ed pieces and articles on the importance and meaning of Date Day and send them free to every Web site and 'zine that reaches that target audience. In the article refer to the book a bit, and include all the contact and ordering information in your e-mail signature. Now Web sites and 'zines all need content. They will take stuff—including excerpts—as long as it's for free. Before we chose this as it . . . any other ideas here?

KELLY: M. J., could he pitch a guest shot? A bit?

M. J. ROSE: Before we look for individual ideas on where he can take it we need to have a big overall strategy—a press kit, a pitch letter and then it has to go out to every single TV show.

BRADLEY: You should try to get it into the script of *The Drew Carey Show*, or have that kind of personality somehow "endorse" the book.

M. J. ROSE: See Bradley, what you and Kelly are doing is thinking specifically. One show won't get the book the kind of attention you need to really sell it. You need a broader overview idea—to get on one show you need to pitch about twenty-four.

PETER B.: My publicist pitches it daily, but M. J. is right. We need a big idea to attract attention, not just a place to pitch it.

M. J. ROSE: Right. A publicist is only as good as the idea, and unfortunately there are a zillion books out there.

BRADLEY: The Date Day idea could be effective in crossing multiple platforms and mediums.

SAC: Dramatic tension always gets me hooked. How about using a kind of "Mystery Man" scenario just to get people interested?

PETER B.: That's an idea, SAC. Who is the man who claims to know enough about sex and dating to write a book on it?

M. J. ROSE: But how do you use it in press? How about if you get a guy to use the book to go out on dates, and you get someone to videotape him and his dates? Then set up a Web site, and run the clips as a kind of soap opera of the handbook in action.

PETER B.: It would take more bandwidth than my site has currently, though that could be easily fixed.

DARKWAYFARER: Are you speaking strictly of e-zines? There are a lot of men's magazines out there.

PETER B.: I've partnered my site with *dateable.com* and *cupid.net,* so far.

BRADLEY: Peter, did you like the comment about print magazines?

PETER B.: My publicist has gone there already, too. As M. J. said, it is hard to get media coverage. Coming up with an idea that creates media coverage is the best idea.

BRADLEY: I like M. J.'s thoughts on getting into something . . . Dan Hurley got onto AOL with his *The 60 Second Novelist.* I think you could find a workable idea of partnership like that, and get into women's Web sites, and forums on AOL. Thoughts?

DARKWAYFARER: I once saw *Men's Health* offer a condensed version of a book on sex techniques. Something like that could really get your name out there.

PETER B.: Writing articles can work, especially if you have credibility.

M. J. ROSE: And to answer the question about print media . . . the way you do this is come up with the pitch and you go after everyone, print, TV, and the Web.

PETER B.: But what about the chicken before the egg syndrome: you can't get publicity without success, you can't get success without publicity.

M. J. ROSE: No, Peter, you don't need success . . . you need an idea that is unique. In an hour we may not get the idea, but you should get a sense of how to look for it. Start by taking a good look at the product, and see how you can exploit it.

WRITEGIRL: Peter said his target audience is women 18–30. What in the book appeals to women? I think that might open the door for a good hook.

PETER B.: Women can either, buy it for men in their lives, or want male psyche perspective.

WRITEGIRL: Neither one of those "feels" very specific . . . sounds too generic for a good hook. I'm thinking of a Sadie Hawkins approach.

M. J. ROSE: Wait a sec . . . we're talking about different things here. When I ask who your target audience is, it's so we know whom the idea should appeal to. But we don't use the target audience as the idea itself or the hook. Follow this logic: The target audience is women who want the guys they go out with to be better dates. That tells us we need to come up with an idea that will get us attention among women who are single, 18–40. Then we come up with an idea and try to get our idea out there in front of that audience. The idea is not what to say about the book but something that is ancillary to the book that will get Peter and the book media attention.

KELLY: I think M. J.'s idea of a contest, or a celebrity date hook is good.

M. J. ROSE: Rule one: Think way bigger than you are thinking. You do not want to get the book on one show. The easiest thing in the world is to come up with a list of what shows you'd like to be on. The effort should be coming up with that one idea.

PETER B.: I think we should pursue the "Date Day" idea. It appeals to women, is unique, and everyone would like to have a special day to go on a date—married and single alike.

BRADLEY: Date Day is the day every woman deserves the perfect date. Peter, all womankind are depending on your book!

PETER B.: Exactly, contests are tough because you need a great medium to promote them. Date Day brings its own promotion and me with it!

M. J. ROSE: Or Peter, you get a great guy who is willing to go on one date for you, and then you get a big Web site to sponsor the Win a Date with So-and-So contest. The date, which will be done by the book, gets covered on the site.

KELLY: Hmmm . . . Date Day you could make "official" too. And Peter, M. J. is right. Some guys *might* say yes. Some big guy might be looking for a promotional *something,* too. Maybe Tom Green.

M. J. ROSE: Remember you are not going to get media coverage unless you have a story behind the book. The guy who used it to win and woo his dream girl. The biggest loser in the world who finally turned his life around.

DARKWAYFARER: M. J., what about a Dater Makeover idea?

M. J. ROSE: How would that get publicity or tie into the book as a story to get you in the press?

KELLY: Peter could run a "Dater Do-over" contest.

M. J. ROSE: That sounds more like an article to me than an promo idea.

KELLY: So what if Peter *wrote* that article?

WRITEGIRL: And marketed it to *Cosmopolitan*?

M. J. ROSE: Sure, Peter could write that article. The simplest way for Peter to get press for this book would be to write about four articles that all tie into the book, get them up on the big Web sites, and pitch others to magazines.

DARKWAYFARER: What if he starts making the guarantee he can make *any* man do better on dates?

M. J. ROSE: I like that . . . now that's a really big idea. Peter, you set up a Web site guaranteeing you can help any man. Then you pick a few men, help them get success stories, and then your publicist takes you and the newly made men on TV shows.

KELLY: And those success stories have both regional *and* national appeal.

M. J. ROSE: It's great. If you go to about.com or a site like that they might let you set it up as one of their sections. Go to *expertcentral.com* and become the date expert. Register yourself and write a pitch letter to their president, and see if they can't set you up. I know the guys there. I might be able to help.

KELLY: Then spread the word . . . become the "Date Expert" elsewhere. The buzz will spread, and suddenly Peter B. and his book will be hot.

M. J. ROSE: You got it. Well I think you saw it work perfectly in here tonight. In an hour we came up with several doable ideas, and by using each other's ideas as jumping-off points we came up with "The One" I think Peter should pursue. Good job, everyone. Peter, become the Date Expert!

KELLY: Great, let's make a date in, say, three months. Peter, will you come back to let us know how the idea worked out?

PETER B.: Absolutely!

2: *HELL TO PAY* BY PETER AZZOLE

KELLY: Pete, tell us a little about your book first.

PETE A: It is a war novel, about a navy pilot during the early months of the Korean War. It has some romance, family conflict, espionage, government corruption . . . in addition to air combat.

KELLY: Great. I'll turn it over to M. J. . . . but feel free to comment, everyone, this is about brainstorming.

M. J. ROSE: Thanks, Kelly. We'll start where I always start. We have to find "The Hook" for the book. The one device we are going to exploit and try to use to get press and promotion for the book. What we look for is the unique thing about the book. Pete, what do you think that is?

PETE A: The title. It seems to evoke curiosity and a vision in all who come in contact with it, particularly in context with the cover image.

M. J. ROSE: I think it certainly is a great title. But you aren't going to get anyone to write an article about you or the book merely because it's a great title. Hopefully every book has a good title. The book is about the Korean War, right? Isn't this year the fiftieth anniversary of that war?

PETE A: Yes, June 25th.

M. J. ROSE: Why not tie your book into the fiftieth anniversary? Do a search for veterans of that war on line. Form a listserv at *onelist.com* for Korean war Vets, and invite them to tell their stories. Put together a press release about the anniversary of the war, include the four or five best vets and their stories, and mention your book. Then send it out to every newspaper and radio show.

Perhaps you could donate 5 percent of all sales of your book to a Korean War memorial fund to help the American public commemorate the war. You'd get press out the wazoo!

PETE A: Okay, I've been doing some of that. My press release starts out that it is the fiftieth, etc., and that this book allows us to relive this pilot's role in that war.

M. J. ROSE: Great start, Pete. But that's a press release for the book. There are a ton of books out there . . . a million press releases.

KELLY: Pete, M. J. is suggesting you create a *bigger* event that might pull your book into bigger arenas.

M. J. ROSE: The trick is to make the news something other than the book . . . make the book an "also." The media needs lifestyle and personality pieces. People sell books. If you can make the war, the fund, and the guys who are still alive the focuses, you will get the kind of press no book alone can get. Reviews and other book press go to the Oprah books and the Stephen King books; we little guys have to get news coverage through another door.

CRAIG: Don't be a novelist, be a journalist and make the news—and embed a reference to your book. Guerrilla marketing.

KELLY: Pete, like your Florida newspaper feature. It was not a review, it was a feature . . . about your iUniverse experience. A bigger story than . . . *just a book*.

PETE A: I put it up on my Web site. I got a full-page feature in the *Palm Beach Post*.

KELLY: M. J. is suggesting you get bigger stories through the Vets angle.

M. J. ROSE: The Vets, a commemorative fund and an unknown author donating some of the money—that's called making a bigger story. But it's going to take work.

KELLY: M. J., isn't it true that a feature is worth around ten reviews? From a publicity point of view?

PETER A: The Navy Memorial in D.C. may just be the ticket. They are cash starved and need some CPR.

M. J. ROSE: A publicist cares much more about features than reviews. And, yes Pete, you got it.

DAVEMAG: There is a Korean War Veteran's Memorial in D.C. as well, near the Wall.

M. J. ROSE: That's heavenly. Plus the papers will love the angle. A cash-starved memorial is the best. Pete, do you have any cash to put into PR? *Hell To Pay*—in honor of all the Vets who are ignored.

PETE A: Not thousands, perhaps hundreds.

M. J. ROSE: Okay . . . all you need is about two hundred to hire a publicist to help you get the press release done the right way and to send it out for you.

CRAIG: Don't forget the ever-popular grant pool.

KELLY: Craig, good suggestion, but Pete's a bit short on time for that process.

M. J. ROSE: First, get to the people who run the memorial, make a proposal to them and get their backing. Ask them for a statement—why they are ignored, what they need, etc.

PETE A: Got it. There are several targets that this would work for. The Naval Air Museum in Pensacola, Florida, would be a great one.

M. J. ROSE: They went to hell and back and no one knows their names— that is a good angle.

KELLY: Pete, there's an Air Force museum in Dayton, too.

PETE A.: Yep, been there and also have that on my list. In fact, I'm a member of all three I mentioned . . . member of one in the UK, too.

M. J. ROSE: I think you have to pick one place and focus on it. But at least you have lots of possibilities.

KELLY: How should the press release be slanted?

M. J. ROSE: Let's brainstorm this one—anyone have an idea for the angle of the release?

PETE A.: Honor the men of the Forgotten War.

DAVEMAG: Remember the men of the Forgotten War.

KELLY: I like that one you said, M. J., "They went to hell and back . . . and no one knows their names. Novelist Peter Azzole thinks it's time to remember."

M. J. ROSE: I like that but we should get the name of the war in there. "Korean War veterans went to hell and back and no one knows their names. Novelist Peter Azzole donates proceeds from his book . . . " etc.

PETE A: Proud men went to hell and back in the Korean War; novelist Pete Azzole helps us honor them.

ASINGER: I think a lot of Vets would like to tell their stories for a press release, but might the stories get kind of long?

M. J. ROSE: The press release would refer to the fact that there are stories available on the Web site. The press release wouldn't give the stories.

KELLY: Right, just the URL.

M. J. ROSE: The Web site would become a repository of personal stories and other information. And the image of the book will be there on the page with each story.

KELLY: But still . . . access . . . accolades . . . Peter gets the glitter.

DAVEMAG: As far as I can see, the stories are the source for another, nearly-ready-made book. *Voices of Forgotten Heroes,* or something along those lines.

M. J. ROSE: Yes, a nonfiction follow-up.

ASINGER: Can I ask a "what if?" What if there aren't enough veterans alive anymore, or the response wasn't so great?

PETE A: There aren't too many, but they are out there.

M. J. ROSE: If there aren't that many Vets alive anymore, you get their kids to tell their fathers' stories.

PETE A.: Oh, the Compuserve and AOL Korean sections of bulletin boards are active.

M. J. ROSE: Yes, use those bulletin boards . . . and use a signature with your messages . . . always. I use the name of my books in my signoff line with my URL.

PETE A: Yep, I've gotten a lot of traffic to the page from bulletin boards. My e-mail signature line with a one-line summary of the book and my URL goes out on every e-mail.

KELLY: M. J., could Peter set himself up as some kind of archivist?

M. J. ROSE: Yes, Kelly . . . if he wants to. But let's stick to the issue of the main effort here. The first step is to contact the memorial of your choice and set up an agreement. Then find a press person to help with the nitty-gritty.

PETE A: I'm doing a book signing at the Pentagon Book Store on April third, any ideas for that?

M. J. ROSE: As to the Pentagon Book store . . . I'd move the signing closer to the June anniversary, so you can use that in relation to all this. If you can't, get working on getting the local press to attend. Send invites to the signing with a release about your plans. Invite local Vets and Vets' kids to the signings, using the Internet to find them. Post every signing on every relevant bulletin board. And when you send out press releases about each signing to the local press in that area, try to get names of some of the Vets who will be at the signings. And get the bookstores to help. Local papers love to do stories on this kind of stuff. And books sell at that level and get buzz.

PETE A: I've already got a reporter from the *Baltimore Sun* coming to the Pentagon. I need to get the *Washington Post* now.

ASINGER: So, the key to book promotion is . . . human interest.

M. J. ROSE: Well, each book is really different. The key to promotion is finding a hook that no one else has used. Yes, Pete, get as many papers as possible. And since the elections are coming up, I'd try to do some fast investigative research and find out if any politicians are Vets or children of Vets. If you do find some prospects, ask each one personally if he or she might show up at the signing or do a radio interview with you.

Don't forget radio in the cities where you are doing the signings, and morning TV. Get them to cover you.

KELLY: And NPR, too. You could approach them with the Korean anniversary tie-in.

CRAIG: What's the key to penetrating the editorial gatekeepers at the big magazines for these press releases?

M. J. ROSE: Getting to them is where the hard work comes in. Phone pitches, e-mail pitches, and snail mail pitches. Plus this is where I'd put the real dollars . . . in getting someone to help who knows some people. But I must say that I did it myself with local papers, radio, and TV, and didn't have a hard time. It's the top big papers and magazines that are tough to crack. But if you keep at it, if just one paper like the *Washington Post* or *USA Today* picks up on it, that's all you need.

KELLY: Okay, let's do a quick recap, a "to do" list for Pete.

M. J. ROSE: 1. Contact memorial of choice to set up fund.
    2. Find cheap but clever PR person.
    3. Send out releases and start work.
    4. Get Vets involved.

5. Update Web site to include all info.
6. Contact all the book stores and get them to help. I found that my local book stores had great press relations and great contact info.

Did I forget anything?

KELLY: Looks great.

31

POPULAR ONLINE PROMOTIONAL TACTICS THAT DIDN'T WORK

M. J. Rose

Just because you build a Web site doesn't mean anyone will come. So how does an entrepreneur with a limited budget attract attention and drive business to her Web site? Not by spending money on promises and letting other people do the work for her.

There are countless stories about people paying thousands of dollars to generate traffic, only to report no sales. Angela Adair-Hoy, on the other hand, is so thrifty that she constantly investigates free promotional tactics and spends nights lying awake, conjuring up creative ways to increase sales. As you will see below, she managed to find free ways to try the same methods that I used. However, her results were as disappointing as mine and, rather than wasting money, she wasted valuable time.

Suzanne Gibbons-Neff, who owns her own public relations company (and unfortunately is more expensive than many of us can afford) said, "I know of two women who spent over $10,000 trying to get Web site visitors without any significant results. Beware of Net marketers. They are out there in full force promising the moon without delivering a single thing."

According to the latest numbers, there are over eighty million Web sites up and running.

Perhaps you can imagine how to advertise your services if you were opening a store on a street that had ten stores, or even one hundred. It starts getting difficult to figure out when there are a million stores on the block. When you start to think in multiple millions, it seems impossible.

That's one reason it's so easy to fall prey to short cuts and "get hits quick" schemes. There is no lack of services promising to drive traffic to your site. I fell for some of them hook, line, and mouse. (And I'm a skeptical New York City advertising maven.)

So look at what I did that failed. Then what I did that worked. Maybe I can save you some money and aggravation.

My goal seemed simple enough: I wanted to get people to my site so they could read a free chapter of my novel and then order a download of the book for $9.95. Not a big ticket item. Plus the book is sexy . . . and they say sex sells best on the Net. So it seemed like a cinch to sell a measly 20,000 books. Maybe even 40,000! I was already checking off houses in the real estate section of the paper.

SEARCH ENGINE SUBMISSION SERVICES

First, I hired a Web consultant who submitted my completed site to over four hundred search engines. Cost: $150. Results: After one month, my site showed up on only five sites. I called and complained and they resubmitted my site to all four hundred sites. After two weeks, my site showed up on ten sites.

Angela's hosting service, Web2010 (*www.web2010.com*), submitted her site to four hundred search engines at no cost. Her results were similar to mine.

OPT-IN E-MAIL LISTS

Next I bought a mailing list of one thousand names of people online that had signed up for and wanted to receive e-mail on the subjects of books. I test marketed three different letters and sent the one that got the best results to the list. Cost: $1,000. Results: Ten percent of all recipients went to the site. Ten percent of those who went there bought the book. Total books sold: Ten books.

Angela considered buying opt-in lists, but after discussing the idea with colleagues who had already tried it, opted not to spend money for sure-fire poor results.

BANNER ADS AND PLACEMENT

I had an animated banner designed. Cost: $300.

I bought banner space on sites that related to my product—fiction and literature. Cost: $1,000. Results: 500 visitors to my site, ten percent bought the book. Total books sold: 50.

I added my site to a mall that promised to generate traffic for me. Cost: $1,000. I then paid more to that mall to list my site as a "hot site" on the mall's front page. Cost: $100 for six months. Results: At the end of four months, I'd had over 20,000 hits to my site, which was impressive. But only 150 visitors had purchased my product.

Angela was surprised by a friend who designed an excellent banner for her. She swapped banners with complementary, yet noncompeting Web sites. Despite the fact that her banner was attractive and said "free issue!" in huge, bold letters, the Web site traffic it generated to *WritersWeekly* *(writersweekly.com)* was almost unnoticeable. So, I'd spent $2,400 to make $1,500. Not great if you care about making a living. Excellent if you are looking for tax loss. I was out almost $1,000.

Now, I not only needed to recoup my investment, but I'd spent all the money I'd put aside for advertising and marketing. And I didn't have any money left. I'd lost my shirt.

It was time to see what I could do without spending a dime.

I figured out the most specific market segment to target. Not just women—that was too broad—how could I reach all women? I chose women who were interested in their erotic selves and women who were avid readers. Then I disappeared into my computer and spent six hours a day, six days a week for three months and searched for e-zines, Web sites, and lists aimed at those two groups of women.

REVIEW COPY RESULTS

I organized the list of sites I'd found from smallest to largest in terms of visitors, or subscribers. I started with the smallest. I wrote to them offering a free review copy of *Lip Service*. At first, only one out of twenty sites took me up on my offer. But those first two gave *Lip Service* great reviews. So, I used those reviews in the next letter I sent out. Little by little, more and more sites wanted to see the book. In four months, thirty sites, 'zines, or Internet newsletters had reviewed my novel.

Angela didn't actively solicit reviews of her books but did investigate and respond to reviewers who asked for free copies of her books. If they owned a legitimate Web site and had a professional presence, she would send them a free copy. They would then post the review on their Web site, which would increase traffic to Angela's site and also sales for her books.

WRITING FREE ARTICLES

Then I wrote three articles. The first was aimed at work-at-home moms about opening a bookstore in the bedroom via the computer. The next, about self-publishing fiction, was aimed at writers. The third article was about not giving up your dreams. In all articles I related my own experiences, with my novel as the focus.

I offered my articles to any site that wanted to use them, for free. All I asked for was a generous signature line (byline) that would give the URL of my site and some information on my novel.

Angela started including a statement in her e-mag saying, "This article may be freely reprinted in its entirety as long as the entire article and byline are included." She started finding her articles (and bylines, which included ads for her books) all over the Net. She subsequently posted all of her prior articles on one Web page where editors and publishers could surf and freely choose which articles they wanted to reprint . . . for free. To see how she markets her free articles, surf to *www.writersweekly.com/angelafeatures.htm*.

JOINING COMMUNITIES AND BEING AN ACTIVE PARTICIPANT

Every day, I read at least two dozen daily digests from all the lists I had joined looking for mentions of new sites or 'zines. I also got involved in discussions on these lists, always signing off with my signature, which included my URL and one line about the book. Once I was an established personality on the lists, the other listmates took interest.

Angela not only participated in other lists, but started one of her own for self-published authors that now has over five hundred professional (and talkative) members.

RESULTS

So after all this, what happened? In the next three months I had only five thousand people visit my site, but I sold one thousand books. Twenty percent of everyone who visited, bought. So, the free PR pulled in better than the paid-for advertising. I had made a big enough profit on the sale of those books to buy more than a few shirts to replace the one I'd lost. Silk, of course.

And what about those search engines? Type M. J. Rose into a search engine like Dogpile or Sherlock, and my name comes up on over fifty different sites. All the places that published my articles or wrote about *Lip Service* did the work for me. That's making the Net work.

32

THE SUREFIRE WAY TO WRITE NEWS RELEASES THAT GET PUBLISHED

Paul J. Krupin

I recently spoke at the National Public Relations Society meeting in Omaha. It was there that I learned most big PR firms don't have a real clue about using the Internet and e-mail to get news coverage.

As editor of Imediafax, a custom news distribution service, I find that most of the people who come to me initially write detailed book reviews or commercial news and Web site announcements, not short articles intended to attract an editor's attention and get published. I often have to tell them to start over or shift gears.

A lot has to do with the content and quality of the book, product, service, or Web site. But let's just assume that you've written the definitive work in your field or a real page-turner of a novel. You have something genuinely terrific to offer. Now what?

A publicity plan!

First, establish your goals for the release. Write them down. Memorize them. Sleep on it. Wake up and think about them some more.

Remember you have to integrate your marketing with your PR and keep it all within your budget.

Let's assume your primary goal is getting the word out about your book. It could be an initial announcement, or part of a year-long monthly campaign to a well-targeted media list (again and again to get name recognition). You've got your schedule and this month your task is at hand. You want to get an article published in as many places as possible to feed sales, acquire name recognition, drive Web traffic, or all the above. These are common goals. You can be more specific, and this will narrow your options and tighten the true alternatives you seriously wish to consider. Think strategically. Narrow the goals and keep it as simple as can be.

Whatever your specific publicity goals, you need to be mindful of the types of news releases that get published. Last April, I completed a qualitative quarterly review of our custom news distribution and the relative success people have had in getting published as a result of sending fax and e-mail news releases. While this is by no means definitive, it is nonetheless useful.

We've seen one-page releases sent to targeted media lists result in successful publicity (defined loosely as having resulted in either wide national publicity, a significant number of top national interviews or bookings, or profit) for book authors, publishing companies, product firms, and government agencies whose one-page news releases took one of the following approaches.

Here's what appears to be working the best:

- **human interest angles**—particularly with heartwarming anecdotal stories.
- **the effect of difficult or controversial issues on interpersonal relationships**—focus on love, sex, money, and the communications between men and women, parents and children, companies and employees, government and individuals.
- **tips articles** . . . advice and tactics excerpted from books, ten commandments, ten tips, etc.
- **unusual events** . . . unique personal accomplishments, unusual creative ideas, humor and wisdom, fun and tragedy.
- **new and unique products or books**—something that hasn't been done before, or a topic that hasn't been addressed, especially Internet innovations and developments.
- **editorial tie-in articles**—holiday and event tie-in articles, and especially politically and socially important issues being raised in the media.

Your chances of success are likely to be increased if you follow one of these formats. Localizing news releases maximizes the potential that your work will receive attention in weekly and daily newspapers. The easiest publicity to get is the announcement of how your book relates to a local event with a distinct human-interest angle.

National publicity is harder, especially in mainstream publications. You compete against everyone in the nation, and you have to distinguish why your news is more worthy of attention than others'.

You can make your job easier and be more successful by breaking your national media lists into geographically distinct areas and localizing the release.

Even once you've identified your target media and settled on a type of news release, it all comes down to writing the actual release. Assuming you are aiming at print (radio/TV releases are a different animal) here's my advice. Bottom line: Find out what works specifically in the media you want to be in.

THE IDENTIFY, IMITATE, AND INNOVATE TECHNIQUE

Go to a newsstand and pick up the latest issues of every relevant magazine or publication you can find, the ones you want to be in. Spend at least fifty dollars. Then dissect each magazine for book articles. Use yellow stickies, or cut the articles out and make a scrapbook. Study the publications closely and see how they write book articles and reviews. Make a list of the headlines. Study the style, length, focus, content, and word choice.

Then start writing by imitating the articles you see. Remember, most of the small articles (which are the easiest to get published) are one page—two hundred words.

Then innovate it. Rewrite it fifteen times. Make it short and snappy. Vary the character of your news release to fit the media you are aiming at.

Remember, you've written the ultimate book in your field. The only book anyone will ever need. Now tell people why in two hundred words. Read it out loud as if you were live on the air—see if it sounds good.

By the way, good short articles in newspapers and magazines are often read on radio stations and on talk shows every day, especially on morning radio talk shows. Listen closely and see if you can tell when it happens. Remember what the radio announcer is doing. He's reading a paper or magazine on the air. Wow—a force multiplier effect. Like being seen on *Oprah* and getting asked to do an interview with *People* magazine.

A news release has to sing to you before you send it out. Take the time to get it right.

There's lots of free information about writing news releases available on the Internet, and more every day. At the Imediafax site *(www.imediafax.com)* you can find plenty of useful links under the title of "On-Line Helpful Articles on Writing Press Releases," as well as information on creating custom media lists.

———————————

Paul J. Krupin is the owner of Direct Contact Media Services *(www.imediafax.com)* and the author of Trash Proof News Releases *(www.publicityforum.com)*.

33

WHERE TO SEND BOOK-RELATED PRESS RELEASES AND ANNOUNCEMENTS ONLINE

Compiled with the help of ebook Connections (www.ebookconnections.com)

About.com's Publishing Page
www.publishing.about.com/business/publishing/library/bl_addebook.htm
Other Web sites add content by drawing from this site's database.

Bookzone.com's Book Flash
www.bookflash.com
Book Flash reports the news about what's happening in the world of publishing, on and off the Internet. New titles, publishing events and announcements, and Internet news—if it's about publishing, it's likely to show up here. News releases appear first in the New Releases section where they stay for thirty days. They are then archived in All Releases, where they'll be available indefinitely.

Bright Ink News
www.klockepresents.com
Monthly newsletter promoting writing world news—new writers, new publications, new books, and more, with special "beware" section.

Cluelass
www.cluelass.com
For mysteries. The Bloodstained Bookshelf lists current releases.

ebook Connections
www.ebookconnections.com

E-mail for news releases and announcements: *news@ebookconnections.com*
Or *editor@ebookconnections.com* (to subscribe, send an e-mail to *ebcmktupdate-subscribe@onelist.com*).
Contact Name and e-mail: Jamie Engle, *jamie@ebookconnections.com*.
All genres.
Format Preferred: text embedded in e-mail, either formal news release or announcement.
Guidelines and Deadlines: Anything e-book or e-publishing related, including publisher news, author news, technology news, industry news, sales/marketing/promotion, special events, contests. Deadline for new book release information is the 25th of the prior month, and needs to be submitted by the publishers to *releaselist@ebookconnections.com* or *editor@ebookconnections.com*. The release list is distributed to other sites.

ebookNet

www.ebooknet.com
E-mail for news releases and announcements: *news@ebooknet.com*
Contact Name and E-mail: Wade Roush, *wade@ebooknet.com*
Genre: Portal site about everything e-book, and weekly e-mail newsletter.
Format Preferred: Plain text.
Guidelines and Deadlines: All e-book- and e-publishing-related material welcome. Deadlines daily. If possible, send releases and announcements a few days before they become public, and they will respect an embargo.

Inkspot.com

www.inkspot.com
Debbie Ridpath Ohi, editor of Inkspot, accepts writing-related news, opinion, or brief press releases for her "Editor Ink" column. "Send them to *editorink@inkspot.com* (put "Letter to the Editor" in the subject header for opinion pieces). Please note that (1) there is no pay, and (2) I cannot guarantee that I'll publish your letter or press release (and please don't ask me to let you know when/if it's published)."

Inscriptions

www.inscriptionsmagazine.com
The weekly e-zine for professional writers welcomes press releases that include information of use to working writers and editors. Please follow these guidelines to properly send your press release. Send your press releases for inclusion in the Publishing News and Notes area to

editor@inscriptionsmagazine.com with the subject heading "News." Speaking online? Giving a book signing? Publishing a great new article or book? Inscriptions would like to promote you and your achievements. Send your press releases to *editor@inscriptionsmagazine.com* with the subject heading "Promotions."

JustViews
www.justviews.com
E-mail for news releases and announcements: *ramsview@northrim.net*
Contact name and e-mail: Brenda Ramsbacher, *ramsview@northrim.net*
Genre: All.
Format Preferred: Body of an e-mail.

The Linguist
linguist.emich.edu/book-policies.html
Announcements must be submitted by publisher, not author.

NetRead's Event Caster
www.NetRead.com/calendar
NetRead's EventCaster broadcasts book and author events to NetRead's subscribers, including fifty major newspapers, plus CitySearch, DigitalCity, and Yahoo's new Literary Events section. The EventCaster is a simple, convenient way to extend book marketing efforts, and it's free.

PRPA
www.topica.com/lists/prpa
E-mail for news releases and announcements: *prpa@topica.com*
Contact name and e-mail: Brenda Ramsbacher, *ramsview@northrim.net*
Genre: All.
Format Preferred: Body of an e-mail.
Guidelines/Deadlines: Must subscribe to the PRPA list before sending a message to the list. ONLY press releases by/for publishers and authors should be sent. To subscribe send an e-mail to *prpa-subscribe@topica.com* or visit the Web site.

Romance Central
romance-central.com
Send news releases and announcements to: *webmaster@romance-central.com*
Contact Name and e-mail: Becky Vinyard, *webmaster@romance-central.com*
Format Preferred: No preference.

Genre: Primarily romance, but interested in all genres and will promote any author/site.

Guidelines and/or deadlines: One or two paragraphs preferred. No deadlines.

Romantic Notions

romanticnotions.com

Send news releases and announcements to: *michelle@romanticnotions.com*

Contact Name and e-mail: Michelle Mar, *michelle@romanticnotions.com*

Format Preferred: No preference.

Genre: Romance with some kind of paranormal or futuristic element, or sci-fi/fiction with romantic elements.

Guidelines/Deadlines: To list upcoming books, include the title, author, publisher, ISBN, publication date, description, and publisher's URL. Submit a month or so before publication, but there are no firm deadlines.

The RunningRiver Reader

www.runningriver.com/readerarchives

Send news releases and announcements to: *news@runningriver.com*

Contact name and e-mail address: Phyllis Rossiter Modeland, *modeland@ runningriver.com*

Format preferred: Can use either a news release or an informal announcement; informality is fine as long as it includes everything.

Genre: All.

Guidelines/Deadlines: Please include written permission—at the same time as the release—to copy book covers and/or author photos from the Web site(s) for inclusion in the archives of the newsletter.

Sharpwriter.com

www.sharpwriter.com

A resource for writers. Has an e-books page.

SoontobeReleased.com

www.soontobereleased.com

A site specializing in prerelease listings and reviews of books, music, movies, and software.

What's New for Book-Lovers at InternetBookInfo.com

www.Internetbookinfo.com

To submit an item to What's New for Book-Lovers, send an e-mail to *ibic@Internetbookinfo.com* with a subject line that contains the string "What's New." Example. "What's New> The Shakespeare Server."

Whispers Online Magazine for Women

www.cyberpathway.com/whispers

Browse under the A&E section for placing your books.

Women International Publishing

www.successforwomen.com

Hosts a directory of published women authors and books that are of interest to women. List your book and Web site free of charge.

Wordbeats Newsletter

www.wordmuseum.com

They have a column called "Shout it from the Rooftops" and interview authors.

E-mail: *wordmuseum@aol.com*

34

PITCHING THE MEDIA BY E-MAIL AND PHONE

Paul J. Krupin

Welcome to the world of electronic commerce. It's amazing but true—you can use e-mail to get publicity with the media. Articles can enhance your visibility, name recognition, reputation as an expert, and position in your industry. E-mail PR is not hard to learn, and the benefits are substantial. But there are some tricks of the trade that are developing in this fairly new marketing technique.

THE GOLDEN RULE: TARGET AND PERSONALIZE

There are several essential rules that publicists must abide by in submitting e-mail to the media if they are to avoid the wrath of the recipients and maintain their reputation as a credible PR practitioner.

TEN COMMANDMENTS FOR SENDING E-MAIL TO THE MEDIA

1. Think, think, think before you write. Ask yourself why you are writing, and what you are trying to accomplish by writing. Put yourself in the position of the person reading your message. You are a busy media professional. What would you do upon receiving your message? Consider it or toss it?
2. Target narrowly and carefully. Go for the quality contacts and not the quantity. Don't broadcast a query or news release or announcement

to irrelevant media. Pick out your target media carefully, based on the industry or readership of the specific media you are targeting. Study the media you are writing to. Write the way the editors write. Make it easy for them to use your submission.

3. Keep it short. Trim your e-mail message so it fills one to three screens. Keep it three to four paragraphs tops. Don't try to sell the media your book. Do try to get their interest so they make a request for more information.

4. Keep the subject and content of your message relevant to your target. It has to be newsworthy and timely. The subject should intrigue them enough to read your message. Present and propose problem-solving articles that advocate the benefits or techniques associated with a strategy, technique, product, or service.

5. If you want to get reviews for a new book, use a two-step approach. Query with a hook and news angle before transmitting a news release or an article, or offer to send a free review copy to those who request it. To avoid angry replies and complaints about unsolicited e-mail, send a very brief e-mail requesting permission to send them a release before actually doing so.

6. Tailor the submission to the media's editorial style or content. Go to a library, read it online, or write and ask for a free media kit and a sample copy of the magazine or journal. Study the style and content of the media. Then write the way they like it. Seek to develop a long-term relationship as a regular contributor.

7. Address each e-mail message separately to an individual media target. Take your time, and personalize each e-mail. Don't ever send to multiple addresses. It's the easiest way to get deleted without being read.

8. Reread, reread, reread and rewrite, rewrite, rewrite before you click to send.

9. Be brutally honest with yourself and with your media contacts. Don't make claims about your book or credentials you can't prove.

10. Follow up in a timely manner with precision writing and professionalism.

Remember, there are real people at the receiving end. Your success with the media, not to mention your credibility and reputation, depends on your respecting the media and being courteous.

It is not hard to garner news coverage if you take your time and do a careful job. The benefits can be phenomenal. E-mail is a good way to make the most of limited funds. You can work locally, regionally, or nationally, and all you need is a computer with an Internet connection and e-mail.

You can and should use e-mail to get news coverage for your business, but you shouldn't rely on e-mail alone. When used together with conventional PR (mail, paper, phone, and fax), you get the maximum effect. Cultivate relationships with media by becoming known as a valuable contributor. If you give them what their readers want, they will give you free publicity.

PITCHING THE MEDIA BY TELEPHONE

Does calling make a difference? You bet it does!

I've been following the direct contact techniques people use to get publicity with great interest as it is a subject very close to my heart. People always ask if calling media, either before or after you send a news release, makes a difference. My own experience is that calling doubles or triples your chances of success. But I decided to find out what the media thinks about this question.

The following are responses to a question I posed in a survey questionnaire to over one thousand radio and TV media executives. The responses were culled to representative responses from thirty-two radio talk show hosts, news directors, show producers, and other media executives. These "straight from the horse's mouth" answers provide extremely valuable insight and guidance about placing those publicity phone calls.

Here is the question:

What is the single most important piece of advice you would give someone who wants to be featured on your show or station? Does calling to speak with you make a difference?

The responses below are just an excerpted portion of my new book, *Trash Proof News Releases,* available in e-book form (*www.booklocker.com/trash*) and soon in print. The media responses overwhelmingly indicate that calling makes a difference.

This first one, by the way, simply illustrates that not everyone enjoys e-mail press releases and related communications.

DEAR PAUL:

I WILL ANSWER YOUR QUESTIONNAIRE WITH THE UNDERSTANDING THAT YOU NEVER SEND ME ANOTHER PRESS RELEASE VIA E-MAIL AGAIN, NOR WILL YOU

DISTRIBUTE MY E-MAIL ADDRESS FOR OTHER MEDIA OUTLETS. I DON'T ACCEPT *ANY* PRESS RELEASES VIA E-MAIL THAT I DON'T ASK FOR. NOW, LEST YOU THINK I'M A REAL WITCH, LET ME SAY YOU MAY INDEED FAX RELEASES TO ME AT 202-XXX-XXXX. JUST NO E-MAILS, PLEASE.

THANK YOU.

MS. MARGIE SZAROLETA, PRODUCER
TODAY IN ENTERTAINMENT HISTORY (AP)

On to the responses!

Al Reinoso, Exec. Producer, *The Rocky Allen Show* WABC, New York

Fax release first and follow up with a call one to two days later. Do *not* call before faxing!

Kevin Jackson, Program Director, KBUN-AM/KKZY-FM

Have something that will directly benefit our listeners.

Eileen Byrne, Talk Host, WLS

Call and say you're sending the information, then send it. Call to follow up but, if you don't hear back, take it as a no, but don't take it personally. Building relationships is key. I may say no to your first try but may really like the next idea you pitch.

Bob Heater, Operations Manager, KKJO/KSFT Radio

Keep it short and to the point. No calls please.

News Director, WSIU-FM, Carbondale, Illinois

If you want us to do a story, you have to tell us how it might matter to our audience. If there's a significance that isn't readily apparent, tell us that in the news release by giving us a contact who can talk about that significance. And make sure you time the mailing so we can get in touch with the contact when we receive the release, especially if the information is time-sensitive.

Calls can hurt your chances of getting coverage, especially when a PR person calls during drive time. I'm a news person. I'm either on the air, getting ready for air, or on deadline. I probably won't have time to talk to you then.

Lauren E. Faulkenberry, News/PSA Director, KWUR (Washington University's radio station)

Calling would certainly help their chances. I receive endless amounts of junk mail and have been known to discard mail from certain addresses without opening it. A telephone call conveys a genuine interest and need.

Ellen Rocco, Station Manager/Program Producer, North Country Public Radio

Write a wonderful book. Don't call me.

Greg Wymer, News Assignment Editor, WFNX-FM

Yes and no. I won't talk to someone who has a bad pitch. One word, though—persistence. Eventually, we all will talk to you.

Katie Leighton, Coordinating Producer

Definitely calling helps. If the person is entertaining on the phone and can charm a producer into using them, they will be looked at and used. Boring topics are one thing, exciting guests are another.

Alicia Maloney, Producer, WQED Pittsburgh

Send info, call to follow up at least twice, and then don't call anymore.

Kristie Credit, News & Public Affairs Director, WOGK K-County 93.7 FM, Gainesville/Ocala, Florida

Send a press release and call to follow up and make sure that we received the information. We get so much sent, faxed, and e-mailed to us that sometimes it does end up in the wrong hands.

Nicholas D. Haines, Executive Producer, Public Affairs/News Programming, KCPT Public Television

Calling does make a difference. It's harder to say no over the phone. But, please remember producers are busy people and one curt response doesn't mean the producer won't be more favorably disposed the next time. We are all interested in providing new and unique content for our program. It would be dumb of us not to listen to any new idea.

Chris Tschida, Executive Producer, A Prairie Home Companion (PRI)

Do not call us. We will call you.

Kimberly Henrie, Vice President/Operations Manager,
Colorado West Broadcasting, Inc., dba KMTS/KGLN Radio

Do your homework. Find out what our audience is and if your product or service will be interesting to these people *before* you call me. Then be prepared to tell me why and how you think there's a match. Because my show is primarily entertainment, I want to know how you are prepared to entertain my audience by sharing your information.

Maria J. Rittenhouse, News Director, Radio, WMCO

Calling and speaking to me definitely makes a difference. It shows that you are interested in our station. We are not just another address on your mass mailing.

David Moye, Senior Associate Editor,
Wireless Flash News Service

Pitch me first before other news outlets and be prepared to tell me the strongest part of your pitch within the first thirty seconds.

Ric Allan, Producer/Host, Digital Village Radio

I never take calls but will call you if interested (so leave a number).

Sue Dieter, News Director, KMRS/KKOK Radio

Answer the question "who cares?" And if it's people in my listening area, I'm more than willing to listen. Direct calls do *not* affect my decision to use releases.

Alice Ikeda, Producer, True Colors

Yes. *Huge.* Paper is paper and when you get fifty of them a day, it all blends together.

Amy King, News Director, 98.7 KUPL, Portland, OR

KISS . . . Keep It Simple and Sweet. Phone calls don't necessarily get you air time. Also, please don't assume that just because you've sent out a press release, it will make it on the air. The event or story has to be something special, something that grabs my attention.

Jana Wyld, Producer/Anchor, KRNV-FM

You must have a sense of humor and lots of patience. People who are super-serious or overly self-important relay those traits to the audience.

Also, our show is formatted in a very loose manner—which means that we don't always get to our guests as quickly as they may wish, hence our adoption of the adage "patience is a virtue." Personal phone calls can be very persuasive—but when a guest or guest-booker is told "no," repeat phone calls can generated bad feelings, as well.

Bob Mallory, News Director, KLBM-AM

Get my name right and get the station's call letters right. I get mailings for people who used to be in my position eight or ten years ago, and I don't use them. It's obvious that they don't care about my station—which they're trying to utilize—if they've never heard of me or don't know what station they're talking to. I field and return every phone call that comes to me—it makes a difference.

C. B. Maxwell, News Director, KNRY-AM 1240

Don't be an egomaniac, don't lie to me, don't feed me a crock of shit, and don't think you are the "only" one with the information. Yes, call me if you dare, but be brief, polite, friendly, and, above all, flexible.

Lorri Allen, News Director, Primedia Workplace Learning

Tell me how it benefits a person in the industries we cover. Calling is fine if I have time—please always ask if I have a few moments before launching into your canned pitch. If you call, give your name, affiliation, and purpose of call and description of service or product in your first sentence. Don't tell me that you are following up on your press release or telephone call. We get thousands of both and reminding me that I don't remember you makes me feel stupid and reassures me that if your call or release was so unmemorable the first time, why should I waste any more time with you on the phone? PR people, put yourselves in our place and life will be a lot easier. If you have the best new gadget that has ever come down the pike, send a sample rather than a multipage BS release describing it.

Jim Roper, Owner, KRTN AM/FM

Keep it short. Lengthy releases cause us to edit and, quite frankly, if it involves much editing, it had better be very important to our area.

Laura Santoro, Public Affairs Director, WRUW-FM Cleveland

Give someone a toll-free way to reach you! This can be an 800 number or an e-mail address. I get so many calls from across the country that, if I returned them all, I would run up a fantastic phone bill. People who have e-mail but then won't use it, and insist that I call them back at their personal number, are placed at the very bottom of my to-do list.

David Hatcher, Executive Producer, Deco Drive

I think a person needs to be straightforward. Don't waste my time by giving me jive about an event or how great this up-and-coming singer is. Just tell it like it is. I like honesty because, if a PR person tells me one thing and the event turns out to be another, I'll think twice the next time I get a pitch. Calling me can work well. I used to be an operator, so I'm very polite on the phone . . . and I do return phone calls. But if I've only talked to you once, don't call back and expect me to remember you, "Hi, David, it's blah blah blah." If you stop there and don't tell me where you're from and what you're pitching, I'm less likely to deal with you.

Jeremy Porter, News Director, KYRO Radio

Calling does help, but is not always the determining factor. In fact, if they call two or three times to hound me about running something that I know my listeners won't care about, that will just turn me off. Again, I would say the main thing is to send me information that my listeners *want* or *need* to know about.

Helene Papper, Sr. News Producer/Anchor, KGOU/KROU, Norman, OK

I don't mind getting phone calls. However it's easier for me to be specific with a person who is looking for coverage if I've read material concerning them. I'd rather call a group or person after I know about them and tell them whether or not I'm interested and the reasons.

Lisa Foxx, On-Air Host/News and Public Affairs Director, KYSR/Star 98.7 Radio, Los Angeles

The best advice I would give would be, *make it sound big!* Treat your press release like a big competition. You don't know what you're up against, so make yours stand out. Never embellish. But be creative. A follow-up call is fine, but again, we are getting five to twenty calls a day from people just like you.

Mike Jaxson, News, Sports, and Public Service Director, KVLC-FM 101.1

Do you have anything my local and regional audience would be interested in? If it's a cookbook on local or regional recipes, chances are I would have that person on the air. If it's someone from New York City wanting to come on the air and talk about his New York City cookbook, chances are I would say no and, yes, calling me in person does make a difference since that person is taking time to speak to me.

Janelle Haskell, Producer, Prime Time and Mature Focus Radio

It's better to have someone call for you—and, yes, calling can make a difference. I don't mind being pitched, if the pitch is to the point and describes the guest and what he/she can really talk about. There is a fine line, however, between pitching and arguing. It's okay to offer reasons why the guest should be on the show, but it's offensive to be argumentative when I express a negative opinion.

Steven Zeigler, Senior Producer, Into Tomorrow

Do some homework. Study our Web site. *Know* what we do. In our case, we are a national/international network radio show, all about home technology and consumer electronics.

Jim Bleikamp, News Director, WFUV-FM Radio, New York

Two things: 1) Acquaint yourself with the nature of the radio station, TV station, or newspaper before you make contact. The station where I am employed, WFUV, happens to be affiliated with Fordham University, but it is not a "college" radio station in the sense that it targets the students in the Fordham campus community. WFUV is actually a professionally staffed 50,000-watt radio station with a weekly cumulative audience of 250,000 bodies, the vast bulk of them in the 25–54 age group. But I constantly get calls from PR people telling me they have a great story for college students. I try to be polite, but sometimes I can't resist saying something like, "That's nice . . . find a station that's targeted at college students." Many PR people don't seem to understand that we are living in an age of growing media fragmentation. For example, almost every radio station in the metropolitan area targets an audience that is somewhat different from other stations. This is also true of cable TV networks—CNN, Lifetime, and E! target very different audiences. 2) It might be best to save the phone calls for your best stuff and, if you do call, get to the point. I don't have time to listen to a one-minute or longer spiel on details about a possible story or guest that I will forget about in another minute anyway. I really think the best pitches are fifteen to thirty seconds. Also save all the editorial comments about how great the guest is. I hear that all the time. I'll be the judge of how great it sounds, and it always sounds greater if it's quick and to the point.

Jim Anderson, News Director, WBDC—WRZR—WAXL, DC BROADCASTING

You don't need to call, just send the info and be available. Disconnect voice mail. *I do not wait.* It's now or never!

Rob Stadler, News Director, WSTR-FM, Atlanta, GA

Calling may make a difference, depending on the guest. The most important advice: persistence! But be prepared to hear no (which I often give to people whose topic just doesn't play into our newscasts or morning show).

Vick Mickunas, Producer/Reviewer/Interviewer, WYSO-FM

Send me the book. Call me once to inquire but don't call me back unless I ask that you do so. I get about thirty nuisance calls every day. Every caller tries to tell me why their book is the most interesting. I always say the same thing: Have you sent me the book? If not, send it to me with your phone number. Don't call me, I will call you if I am interested. My program is in very high demand. I turn down twenty guests a day.

35

SPEAKING ENGAGEMENTS

Angela Adair-Hoy

Public speaking is an excellent way to promote your book while getting paid and a free trip to boot. I was recently paid $500 to talk for thirty minutes and ended up selling several dozen copies of my book on CD-ROM in the hour after my speech. Nice!

But how does one get speaking engagements? Here's a super site. Don't skip this one: *www.shawguides.com.*

You can also scan the search engines for conference+your specialty. E-mail the conference organizers and offer your speaking services at their next conference. Most conferences are annual, but there may be plenty for you to choose from.

WHAT TO TAKE

Carry enough books (put e-books on disk or CD-ROM) to sell to interested attendees. I always take enough to sell to at least 25 percent of the attendees. If you run out, that's okay. Simply direct your unfulfilled customers to a place where they can order your book online.

DECLINING SPEAKING ENGAGEMENTS

I was recently invited to speak for the National Management Association on self-publishing. I turned them down. First, how many professional managers are likely to start writing or self-publishing? Second, the gig was local and didn't give me the chance to see a new town. And they weren't going to pay me anyway. Consider each invitation carefully. If the audience is a likely target for your book, then go for it, even if they don't pay you. But the conference organizers *must* pay for travel and accommodations.

If you don't know anything about public speaking, buy *Speak and Grow Rich* by Dottie and Lilly Walters. It's fabulous!

36

BOOK SIGNINGS: NOT BY THE BOOK

M. J. Rose

I am sitting behind a table in the front of a bookstore in a suburban mall. Lined up in front of me, like good soldiers, are twenty pristine copies of my novel. I've been here for forty minutes and only four people have wandered over to the table. Three to ask if I know what the newest *Oprah* selection is. One to ask me the time. No one has even picked up my book.

So I've capped my pen and am trying to figure out what's gone wrong with this book signing.

A decade ago an author showing up at a bookstore was guaranteed to attract a crowd. But these days book signings are nothing novel. According to one publisher (who asked to remain anonymous) only the biggest names attract a significant crowd anymore. The plot gets even more depressing when you look at the price of national book tours. They have become so expensive publishers are willing to send only their biggest draws. Which leaves 70 percent of authors to set up these events for themselves.

There are some tried and true methods that can help draw a crowd. (I wish I'd known them in advance.) There are also some alternatives to doing signings altogether.

"I found several things worked to attract people to signings," said Mike Shockey, author of *Seized* and *Ravager*. "Along with very professional posters displayed two weeks in advance, I found that bringing a television and running a TV interview really attracted people. This, along with flyers both in the stores and in mailboxes in the area, made a big difference."

In my case, the bookstore's manager simply forgot to post anything in advance about my coming. This being my first signing, I didn't think to call him two weeks in advance and remind him. Next time you can be sure I will. But what else can an author do?

Robin Bayne, author of *His Brother's Child* and *The Will of Time*, suggests having a multipublished author sign along with a newbie. "I did my first event with Mary Jo Putney, and it was great," said Bayne. "The questions were directed to both of us; we each gave our own version of answers." Bayne feels having another, more experienced author there not only helped sales of her book but also helped relax her.

"And if no one had shown up, at least I would have had another author there to talk to," added Bayne.

Romance author Pauline B. Jones said, "The biggest draw for me so far has been buying the Rocket eBook and bringing it with me to the signing. It's like a people magnet."

Another magnet is food, said Connie Correia Fisher of Small Potatoes Press. "For our cookbook, *PB&J USA,* we have held 'make your own PB&J' contests for kids (and had one for adults, too) and had nationally known chefs do PB and J demonstrations."

The wackiest thing Fisher ever did was have a huge PB&J booth outside of a major bookstore on the Saturday before Christmas. "Our idea was that shoppers would need energy. We made over two thousand PB and J combinations with different kinds of jelly, five different breads, and hundreds of toppings and fillings from fruit to goobers, plus an amazing amount of peanut butter, plain and crunchy, of course."

Yes, there are creative ways to entice readers to signings, but the Internet offers a virtual alternative to brick-and-mortar book signings.

Instead of spending $2,000 on planes, car rentals, hotel rooms, and meals, the money can be spent on a book marketing firm that specializes in setting up virtual book tours. These firms book author chats on large sites like AOL, iVillage.com, and TalkCity.com, to name a few.

If you don't have the money to hire a firm, there are hundreds of smaller chats you can get yourself booked on. Just check out the book club section of all the major sites. You may not get front-page coverage announcing your chat, but the hosts do make an effort to announce the event to several hundred people.

Get acquainted as a participant first. Get the feel of the site. Get to know the hosts and then e-mail them and tell them about your book. I've found most of these hosts are real book lovers and are extremely kind to authors.

From the comfort and convenience of your home office (or even your bedroom), you can meet and greet virtual fans and sell the same twenty books you would have sold at your local Borders or Barnes & Noble. (Or in my case, sell twenty more books than I did at that mall bookstore).

At least in the chat room, the host will be there if no one else comes. Whereas at the bookstore, if no one shows up, there's not much you can do except sit down and write an article about it.

37

THE BOOK PARTY COMES TO CYBERSPACE

M. J. Rose

It was another of those dreams I'd held on to—having a book party when my first book was released. I imagined the waiters with trays of champagne and wine, the mingling guests, the press who would ask me what my inspiration was—you know the fantasy, I'm sure.

Well, my first book party was and wasn't quite what I'd imagined. First of all, it wasn't in a chic restaurant or in my editor's home in Manhattan. It was in cyberspace and it was held in a chat room. But it was free and fun and a great promotional tool that anyone can use to generate attention.

WHAT IS A CYBERBOOK PARTY?

Like any book party it's a celebration to announce the publication of a book. It's a wonderful way to sit back for an hour, have some fun, thank your friends for putting up with you while you were writing the book and just plain revel in the fact that your book is finally out there and available.

But it's also a great way to get some local and Internet press and introduce new readers to your book.

As with a traditional book party it's best to send out invitations—but with a cyberbook party they go out via e-mail, of course. And it's a good idea to have free books on hand to give out to the partygoers.

Now, in non-virtual space the books would be paper and ink, but at a cyberbook party they are electronic files that get sent to the partygoers via the Net.

Certainly invite friends and relatives to the party, but also other authors, readers, and, most important, the press.

I was lucky enough to have a reporter from Salon.com come to my cyberbook party, and if you'd like to read Heidi Kriz's take on what it was like, it's archived at the Salon Web site, *www.salon.com/business/feature/2000/06/01/bookparty/index.html*.

HOW TO SET UP YOUR PARTY

You have a few choices. You can have a private party in a chat room that your server provides. For instance, if you are a member of AOL, you can host the party in a private chat room or a public one. The benefits of doing it this way are that it's easy and it's free.

The drawbacks are that there's usually a limit to how many guests (twenty-five) can be accommodated, and you probably won't be getting AOL, or your particular provider, to do any promotion for you.

The other option is to find a Web site that has chat capabilities. Look for a site that also has some connection to your title.

For instance, if your book is about a military man involved in a murder, contact someone with a big military Web site and ask the host if he or she would like to host the party. Explain the concept to the host, pointing out how he or she could use it to generate traffic and build buzz about their site.

One site I suggest you look at is *www.about.com*. There are over seven hundred sites within that site, each on a very specific topic, and each with chat facilities.

So for example, if you've just written a romance that takes place in the South of France, contact the French About.com guide and ask if she'd like to have the party there. Offer her the chance to invite her visitors and tell her you'll be bringing your own friends and fans.

What will she get out of it? All the new people you'll be bringing to her site for the first time. Plus a new event that she can use to generate traffic.

What will you get out of it? Exposure on a site you may not have been able to get exposure from before.

A third place to have a cyberparty is where I had mine: The Book Report (*www.bookreporter.com*). This site is dedicated to readers and books. And their chat facility allows for over one hundred guests, so chances are—unless you are Stephen King—none of your friends or fans will be turned away.

The benefit of having your book party at The Book Report is that they will promote it among their audience of readers. So you'll be reaching exactly the kind of folks you want to be reaching. The only thing is that The Book Report charges for hosting a book party. Not as much as champagne and canapés would cost you at a real party, but they do charge. But you get quite a bit for your money.

The Book Report has over fifty thousand visitors a month who will be hearing about the party. Plus the party will be mentioned in a special newsletter The Book Report sends out to subscribers weekly. Even if they don't come, all those people will be reading about you and your title. This is key—every mention of your name and the name of your book counts. This is a cheap way to get some great advertising.

Another benefit of having The Book Report host your party is that they will provide you with a host who will field questions, keep the party moving, get the conversation going, spout interesting tidbits about your book (the host will read the book prior to the party) and generally make sure everyone has a good time.

PRE-PLANNING

Before every party there are important steps to take. Usually it's whom to hire to cater the event and what band to hire. In this case you need to make sure you already have reviews of the book. (See our chapter on Getting Reviews). You'll need the reviews so you can send out review blurbs with the invitations to readers and the press. And so the host can mention the reviews and possibly post a line or two from them during the chat.

In advance of the event, some authors create little icons from letters and characters to use during the party. Cyber champagne glasses can be created from the capital letter Y with quotation marks over the v. Hors d'oeuvres can be made from O's. Be creative—there are no limits or restrictions. Other authors I know have electronic autographs made by scanning their signature into a PDF file and then offering them to the guests.

One of the best suggestions is to make sure you have a host—even if you draft a friend to do it. You can't brag about your own book, but your host can.

Work with the host to make sure he or she has questions to ask you if the party hits a snag, such as—"What was the best fan letter you got so far?" Or just "Tell me how you feel now that the book is finally out."

THE INVITATION

First you've got to write one. Here's what I sent out for my cyberbook party.

I'M PROUD TO ANNOUNCE THAT POCKET BOOKS IS RELEASING THE E-BOOK OF *LIP SERVICE* (WHICH HAS JUST BEEN CHOSEN BY SUSIE BRIGHT TO BE IN-CLUDED IN *BEST AMERICAN EROTICA 2001*).

TO CELEBRATE YOU ARE INVITED TO THE FIRST EVER "CYBERBOOK PARTY" HOSTED BY THE BOOK REPORT (WWW.BOOKREPORTER.COM). PLEASE COME AND HELP MAKE THIS A FUN EVENT. WE WILL BE GIVING AWAY 50 FREE COPIES OF *LIP SERVICE* AS WELL AS ONE ROCKET READER.

WHERE: IF YOU GO TO: (CLICK HERE) TBR CHAT: BOOKACCINO AND THE BOOK STORY YOU WILL FIND A SPECIAL LINK WHICH WILL LEAD YOU TO THE PARTY. WHICH IS KEYWORD TBR AT AOL.COM. (YOU WILL NEED AOL ACCESS TO ATTEND)

WHEN: MAY 16TH AT 10PM EST (ONLINE OF COURSE.)

HOPE TO SEE YOU ALL THERE,
M. J. ROSE

What to Include

Of course you've got to put in the where and the when. But you've also got to give the book a bit of spin. And it doesn't hurt to offer prizes. Yours don't have to be the same as mine.

If your book is a nonfiction book on the Best Restaurants for Kids at Disney World, the prize can be a $50 gift certificate to the best restaurant for kids at Disney World. Or the prizes can just be copies of your book.

HOW TO GET THE PRESS TO COME

Now chances are *The New York Times* won't cover your cyber party, but that doesn't mean you can't get press. First, think locally. You have a home-town newspaper, local radio stations, and local TV stations. Send them press releases and invitations. Give the party a hook.

If it's a horror book about vampires and witches, have the book party on

Halloween. Chances are at least one member of the fourth estate will think this is an interesting sidebar to run on All Hallows' Eve. If it's a wonderful mother/daughter saga, hold the party on Mother's Day and invite mothers to bring their daughters and vice versa.

Remember when you give the press the hook or an angle it makes their job easier. Local reporters are always looking for interesting local stories and e-books and the Internet is still very newsworthy. Don't just send the press release and invitation—please follow up with phone calls and speak to the reporters yourself. You have a much better chance of getting some coverage if you talk to them on the phone.

Don't Forget Online Press

Contact all the e-zines, online reporters, and columnists you can think of. Search out who writes about mother/daughter relationships for iVillage. Who runs the women's page at AOL? Do searches on search engines for large Web sites on your topic and write to the Webmasters inviting them and their audience to come to the chat. The About.com guide to relationships might be very interested.

Also be sure to give away free e-books to the press you are trying to interest in showing up. If they like the book they'll be that much more likely to attend.

One word of caution—don't attach the e-book to the invitation. The press deletes mail that contains attachments due to worries about viruses. So ask if they'd like a copy of the book and then send it on.

Word of Mouth

Tell your friends to pass on the invitation. Mention the party on the discussion boards you frequent or the listservs you belong to. Don't be shy. Not everyone will come so you do want to over-invite.

Most of all, enjoy your party.

Don't get over-involved in the idea that seventy-nine people have to show up and buy the book. Everything works synergistically in promotion. Just one reporter who shows up to your party could be impressed enough to keep you in mind for a feature the next time your local paper writes an Internet story.

38

SITES THAT HOST AUTHOR CHATS

The following is a list of sites that host author chats. Some sites are interested in books of all types, while others are genre specific. Surf to these sites to find out what they offer.

About.com
home.about.com/arts/index.htm
Click on "They're chatting about . . ." in lower right-hand column

America Online
www.aol.com

Barnes & Noble.com
www.bn.com/community/community.asp

The Book Centre
www.osiem.org/chatschedule.htm
Spiritual books

CNN.com
cnn.com/chat

CompuServe
www.compuserve.com

Delphi
www.delphi.com

Hay House
hayhouse.com/chat/default.htm
Personal empowerment books

iUniverse
chat.iuniverse.com/default/default.asp?nick=&channel=

NBC Talk City
www.nbc.talkcity.com/communities/art_books.html

NovelTalk
www.debstover.com/chat.htm

Romance Central
www.romance-central.com/chat.htm

Romance and Women's Fiction Exchange
romex.dm.net/chat.html

WordMuseum
www.wordmuseum.com/chat.htm

Wordsworth.com
www.wordsworth.com

World Without Borders: Author! Author!
worldwithoutborders.com/calendar/author.html

The Writer's BBS
www.writers-bbs.com

Writers Hall Writers and Readers Chat
www.geocities.com/SouthBeach/Cove/3364/chat.html

Writerspace
www.writerspace.com/chat

Writers Write
www.writerswrite.net

Yack.com
www.yack.com

Yahoo!
chat.yahoo.com/?room=books@entertainment

SITES WHERE YOU CAN CREATE YOUR OWN CHAT FORUM

Delphi
www.delphi.com

Slake.com
www.slake.com

39

CONDUCTING TARGETED "TRAVELING" MEDIA PUBLICITY TOURS

Paul J. Krupin

You do not have to travel one hundred fifty days a year to be a successful author or publisher. Neither do you have to get up in front of people and speak. Instead, you can make "appearances" on radio and in print media day in and day out from home. A reasonably well-designed custom-targeted publicity campaign can bring you from city to city, day after day.

Sure, you may have to be willing to travel a little, especially for major media appearances. But I work with lots of authors, publishing companies, and publicists who arrange for nationwide media tours with the author sitting at home on the telephone in his office, or at the kitchen table in her bathrobe at four A.M. Pacific Standard Time. (That's seven A.M. Eastern Standard Time . . . morning talk radio prime-time on the East coast).

Tim McCormack of Green Tree Publishing successfully launched a month-after-month print and radio campaign that resulted in hundreds of articles and talk show interviews all over the country, resulting in major book sales. For Dr. Sal Severe's book, *How to Behave So Your Children Will, Too,* Tim created and sent out one-page human interest news angle releases that keyed in on national current events. The news releases were sent out to two thousand media outlets nationwide, month after month after month.

You don't have to conduct a major nationwide campaign to be successful, especially if you can't afford the time and money needed to maintain the effort at that level. You can reduce the number of media outlets you contact each time and go with a lower-cost effort.

The way to conduct a "road tour media campaign" is to create a media outreach schedule that walks from state to state, market area to market area, or from city to city, across the country. The level of effort (that is, the number of media contacts and hence cost), can be set at whatever level you can afford.

You can skip the major metropolitan areas, and zero in on the midrange markets and cities. If you are working with the midrange media markets, the total number of radio shows, radio stations, TV shows, TV stations, and daily and weekly newspapers can easily number a total of one hundred media contacts per city. And at just a few cents per faxed page, your publicity costs are minimal. If you landed one or two interviews and a single article, it would probably be a profitable venture.

Create one well-written news release offering both content and substantive information or tips so you address print media editor interests. Also indicate what the author can talk about and why people will be interested in the subject and author so you address the needs of radio shows, radio stations, and TV show producers and guest hosts in the selected target areas.

This next point is of critical importance. The real key to being successful in a city-by-city campaign is thinking hard and creating a local news angle for the news release. Many authors have a book subject with broad national interest or appeal. This will get some editors thinking about an invitation or an article, but it will not get as many as when there is a distinct local news angle highlighted in the news release.

A local news angle is one that features a local citizen, event, activity, problem, concern, or benefit. Thus, if you send a news release to New Orleans media, the release should contain something of specific interest to people in that community.

This can be one of the most difficult ideas to implement effectively. It often takes some real creativity if you don't know anyone who can act as a local focal point or subject of interest. So brainstorm and do some research. Use the Internet and phone book to identify a local participant who would like to share some publicity with you. Then call someone, or a company or organization, to ask if they will participate. You can call ahead and make the arrangements, get the quote, the local case study, or problem analysis. Get a local to review the book, say how they used it in solving a problem, or helping someone, or just how they enjoyed it. Send your request to the mayor, or to a principal, or president of a volunteer organization, or charity, or self-help group. Do what you need to do to come up with a hard local news angle.

You use the local news angle in each "local" news release. Once you come up with a formula, you duplicate it city by city.

Editors love when you do this for them; it saves them work! The media response rate for news releases with a local news angle is the highest of any type of news release I send. You get more interviews and more publications.

Of course, you can always travel. A local event, like a book signing or a workshop, makes it easy, especially if it is part of a mini author tour.

Getting publicity for mini author tours is easy with a good action plan. It often makes the difference between a humdrum event and a supersuccessful event with lots of associated book sales.

Here are some of the lessons I've picked up from conducting publicity campaigns with fax and e-mail for authors and publishing companies, using the Internet to Imedia Fax service (*www.imediafax.com*).

Follow these steps to plan, implement, and leverage publicity before, during, and after a mini author media tour:

1. Lay out your tour schedule identifying points of contact that will work both in advance of the event and while at the event, so media can contact you beforehand and on short notice.

2. Create a custom targeted media list covering the daily and weekly newspapers, news services and syndicates, radio and TV stations and shows in the market areas of your event locations. Research and consider sending the release to magazines in the market areas because that can result in publicity with a long-term effect, long after the event.

3. Prepare a one-page release describing who, what, where, when, why, why it is important, why it's going to be a great event, and whom to contact. You can use one press release per location or one press release for multiple locations, depending on how you select your media list and transmission schedule. Make sure you localize your news release to the maximum extent possible to show the media the event has significant local readership and editorial interest.

4. Send out your first news release three weeks before the event. For daily and weekly newspapers, target the calendar editors, metro editors, and the feature editors.

5. Follow up by phone with the most important media outlet on your list at each location, to achieve coverage of the event and to invite the media to attend or interview the author before, at, or even after the

event. Invite feature editors to come to the event, and offer tailored articles, interviews, and site visits if your schedule allows.

6. Send out a second news release seven to ten days before the event, and follow up once again to get and confirm media attendance or interviews.

7. Conduct the event and do the interviews. Treat the media in attendance in a very special way. If they came in response to your release, thank them and make it worth their while. Give them review copies if you haven't already done so. Be quick to take advantage of an opportunity to get more publicity or better media coverage.

8. Send out a final news release immediately after to leverage the success of the event. The event itself is news. This release should be a short article which summarizes the high points of the event and provides book ordering and contact information.

9. Call to thank the media contacts for the coverage and to request tear sheets (actual copies of the part of their publication where your article appeared). Offer additional information, articles, or interviews by phone as appropriate.

BOTTOM LINE

You can reach out and touch people across the country quite easily if only you create a plan and implement it. It's not hard to do, and it need not cost an arm and a leg.

You can see numerous examples of news releases being used for road tours, bookstore signings, and speaking engagements at the Direct Contact News Wire site at *www.dcnewswire.com.*

40

GETTING REVIEWS

Written with Jamie Engle

Each time I got a good review from a site, e-zine or newsletter, I asked the author of the review for permission to post it to Amazon.com and Barnes&Noble.com. As the number of reviews grew, so did sales.

BUDGETING

A majority of reviewers, especially offline, prefer printed review copies. If you're publishing in electronic format only, sending print copies increases your publishing expenses. Reviewers who accept electronic formats may require "hard copies" on diskette or CD-ROM, rather than an e-mail attachment, download, or browser viewing. Labels, cases, disks, postage, and stationery supplies are expenses you'll need to include in your budget.

PREPARING A REVIEW PACKAGE

Prepublication reviews and postpublication reviews are sent to different reviewers. Send clearly marked advance review copies (ARCs) for prepublication review packages.

Marking e-book editions can be tricky. Include the title or a recognizable abbreviation and, if it's an advance copy, the letters "ARC" in the file name. For example, "MyBookARC.doc." Inside the file, put "advance review copy" on the first and last pages. This way, if a reviewer uses book-marking and skips the cover page when opening the book, they're reminded it's an advance copy at the end of the book.

Submission guidelines will usually tell you what file format is preferred. If not, use TXT (text), RTF (rich text format), or HTML. These formats are compatible with most machines. Many reviewers are using Rocket eBooks for reviewing e-books and prefer HTML because it keeps more formatting upon RocketEdition conversion.

Your review request should be prepared according to the reviewer's submission guidelines. In general, the request should include pertinent book information and an offer to send the book for review upon request. Do not attach the e-book file unless submission guidelines specifically request file attachments. Fear of computer viruses prevents most sites from accepting file attachments. Book information to include is:

Title
Author and URL
Publisher and URL, address, e-mail, fax number
Publication month and year
ISBN(s)
Formats available
Delivery options available
Price
Where available for purchase
Estimated number of pages or number of words
Genre/subgenre
Short book summary
Short review quotes
Short author bio

RESEARCH

If you are going through a publisher, ask them where they will send your book, then you can fill in from there. It's expensive and time-consuming to send books to every book reviewer available. To save money and time, make sure the reviewer or publication has an interest in your book. Rank publications by how closely their audience matches your book's audience, number of subscribers, and other promotion opportunities available at the site or publication. Search out the review sources less in demand, where there's less competition for attention. Expand the number of reviewers available by looking offline and online.

Be sure to note the review request guidelines and follow them exactly.

PLANNING A CONTINUING PROGRAM

E-books have a longer shelf life, giving you more promotion time. Spread your review requests out so that new reviews are being released throughout the shelf life of your book instead of all at once. You won't be able to control it completely; reviewers can take anywhere from a few weeks to a couple of years to review your book. But you can try to help things along by sending your book out in batches. First send it to those most likely to review it. Then, once reviews start coming in, send it out to the second batch of reviewers.

Always be on the lookout for new review publications and sites. You'll find them by networking with other authors and readers, and some good old-fashioned Web surfing.

TRACKING AND FOLLOW-UP

Keep track of when and where you send your book and follow up as necessary. Include the information you need to follow up on your request: name, publication or Web site, URL, address, e-mail, phone number, fax number, date sent, date of follow-up, date review received.

If no response to your initial request is received, it's standard to follow up and make sure the request was received. If the guidelines say reviews take about eight weeks, you can follow up in about eight weeks. Any more than that and it might be considered hounding the reviewer, especially if they've had a bad day.

USING REVIEWS RECEIVED

In your follow-ups, be sure to include review quotes from other reviews received. It lets the reviewer know others are reacting favorably and the book rates a second glance. Be ethical when pruning these gems, however; don't change the intention of the reviewer's words by overzealous editing.

Update your promotion materials, book listings, and Web site with new review quotes. If the review is from a prominent publication or reviewer, perhaps a news release is in order. Don't by shy about spreading the good reviews you're getting—they're one of the best sales tools you have!

GETTING LOCAL INK

If you think getting online pixels is tough, getting offline ink is even harder. But like everything else, if you approach it the right way, you can do it.

The first place you want to start is at home. Chances are the town you live in has both local newspapers and local cable shows. And they are always looking for local stories. So turn yourself into one.

Find a hook in your story. You won't get any press if your hook is "I wrote a book." You need to give the reporter something to bite on. Some ideas:

- Even though there are thousands of authors selling their work online, chances are that in your little town you are one of the few. So make that the pitch. "Local author takes to the Internet to sell her book."
- If your book takes place in your town, use that as the angle. "Book about Your Town, USA, to debut on the Net."
- If you have gotten great online press already, make that the angle. "Local author interviewed on major Web site."

You get the idea—it's not that different from finding the USP for your book. To attract the attention of the press, you need to come up with a unique selling press opportunity.

Write up a press release and send it to every local editor of each newspaper, magazine, or TV station that does local lifestyle news. Morning shows are great for this if your town has its own. Don't try *The Today Show* or *The New York Times* until you've got a really *big* story.

Another way to get local press is to go to your local bookstore and offer to do a reading and a demonstration of an e-book reader. Have your e-book burned onto CD-ROMs so the local store will have something to sell and make sure you alert the press to the demonstration.

E-books are in the news all the time now. Local bookstores are very open to demos of this kind. One woman I know has been doing every local bookstore in her area and pulls in crowds of fifty or more for each demo. She also sells about three dozen CD-ROMs every time.

41

HOW TO GET YOUR BOOKS REVIEWED OFFLINE

A few months ago, Paul J. Krupin conducted a survey of 1,300 book review editors for print publications across the United States. Before you see the results, it is really helpful to understand what the universe of book reviewers in the United States looks like. At the time he did the survey, there were:

Daily Newspapers—Book Review Special Sections: 53
Daily Newspapers—Book Review Editors: 512
Weekly Newspapers—Book Reviews Editors: 2
Magazines—Book Review Editors: 911
Magazines Without a Book Review—Editors that Do Book Reviews: 4,982
News Services and Syndicates—Book Review Editors: 40
Syndicated Columnists—Book Review Beat: 32
Radio and TV Shows that Focus Exclusively on Books: 10
Specialty Book Review Magazines with Feature/Managing Editors/Editors (some without book review editors): 29
Total in All U.S. Media = 1,569 Book Reviewers

While Paul believes this is still probably conservative, this is still a lot of book reviewers.

Paul conducted a survey questionnaire via e-mail. He asked over 1,300 editors fourteen questions and received 144 detailed responses. Below are some of the results in response to one key question.

Since getting reviewed is the first step in getting publicity, he asked: "What is the single most important piece of advice you can give authors who wish to get reviewed?"

Ben Pappas, Lifestyle Editor, *Forbes* magazine
"For *Forbes,* there is no set way. Read the magazine and take tips from previous books that have been reviewed in terms of what topics will work."

Christopher Sterling, Book Review Editor,
Airways and Communications
"I enjoyed filling this out—and wish you well. You have put your finger on a crucial failing in the publishing industry—getting information on new books into reviewers' and thus readers' hands. As a long-time reviewer in two specialty areas, this has long been a problem."

Alan Caruba, Editor, *Bookviews* (monthly newsletter)
"Authors have to understand that more than 50,000 books are published annually and most are sheer rubbish. They need to find, identify, and promote the hell out of the most unique aspect of why their book is different, special. For a reviewer, it becomes déjà vu very quickly after you've seen a thousand cookbooks, travel memoirs, etc.!"

Glenn Abel, Executive Editor, *The Hollywood Reporter*
"Know the publication and its audience."

Dan Webster, Books Editor, *The Spokesman-Review*
(Spokane, WA)
"Tell me why my readers, the people of the Inland Northwest, should be interested in reading your book. And then arrange a reading stop in Spokane and/or Coeur d'Alene."

Robert Schildgen, Managing Editor, *Sierra* magazine
"Don't waste your time trying to get somebody to review a book that is of a kind or on a topic that the publication rarely or never reviews. Target your efforts to the right magazines."

Richard Nicholls, Literary Editor, *The American Scholar*

"Draw up annotated lists of publications likely to be responsive to your book, and make sure that you go over the list with your publicist. Then follow up to make certain that review copies have in fact gone out to the publications you feel are most likely to be responsive. If you believe particular publications need to be specifically flagged about your book, tell your publicist why this must be done, and what kinds of things should be said."

Michelle Pilecki, Managing Editor, *Pittsburgh* magazine

"Don't wait until you have finished copies to start the review process. That's way too late for most publications. And with the megachains giving books only six weeks on the shelves, your book is on the remaindered table before it ever gets a chance of a review."

A. J. Hamler, Associate Editor, *Woodshop News*

"Get it to me, the sooner the better. I don't want to have it in the magazine months after every other magazine has done it."

Rebecca A. Stewart, Associate Editor, *Journals*, International Reading Association

"A good press release is vital. It doesn't have to be long, but be *sure* that all the information is correct, and proofread it several times. It is a complete turn-off to get a press release containing misspelled words."

Susan Daniels, Associate Editor, *Quality Progress* magazine, the American Society for Quality

"For our magazine, it's simply whether it is about a topic which relates to the quality field and perhaps breaks some new ground."

Cheryl Scott, Associate Editor, *BioPharm*, Advanstar Communications

"Do your research. Don't just look at the name of a magazine or some short description in a guidebook and send your stuff en masse. At the very least, check out a magazine's Web site, which should be able to give you some idea of its focus and approach. Find out who its readers are, and only send your proposals to those magazines that specifically address your subject area. The magazine arena is becoming more and more niche-oriented, and authors and PR types need to be aware of that. And they need to approach us accordingly."

Thomas Burns, Publisher/Managing Editor, *Northern Breezes, Inc.,* and *Sailing Breezes*

"Write well-researched material. Even if it's fiction, my instruction to reviewers is that if it involves sailing or the sea in some form, you, the reviewer, must look at the material for accuracy and sensibility. For example, I saw this once in a children's fiction book, '[The character] was sailing downwind in ten knots of breeze at eight knots with the seas on the beam, the finish in view straight ahead and the wind in her face . . .' This is the problem: In ten knots of breeze going downwind, the seas are in back of you not on the beam. And if the boat is really going eight knots, there is at most two knots of breeze anywhere on her body and it would be on the back of her neck, not in her face. I don't know how you ever got me to write this much! I hope it is of some use to you."

Milton Moore, Arts Editor, *The Day* (a daily newspaper), New London, CT

"For *The Day,* just 'don'ts': Don't write about self-help. Don't write about angels. Don't write about TV personalities. We have *The New York Times* and Knight-Ridder wire services which give us many excellent reviews. However, I will often be alerted to a book by perusing or reading the review copy. The best case in point is *Wind-Up Bird Chronicles* which I thought was one of the books of the year, but it received little buzz. When a *Globe* review finally moved, I ran it on a section front, because I had read the book (on vacation, without taking notes). Mail it to me with bio info. I find *Publishers Weekly*–type blurbs uniformly upbeat and useless."

Morley Walker, Entertainment Columnist, Book Review Editor, *Winnipeg Free Press*

"Write a great book and get published by a major Canadian publisher."

Frank Moher, Contributing Editor, *Saturday Night*

"Well, unfortunately, the best bet is to get published by a big, mainstream publisher; the small publishers still have trouble getting their books attended to (although I try to mitigate this as best I can). Beyond that, it's largely a fish shoot, depending on editorial mix, timeliness maybe, and editor's taste. Just write."

Arthur Salm, Books Editor, *San Diego Union-Tribune*

"We try to be eclectic, informative, and interesting. But I could take our section from any week, scrap it, and put out another section just as worthy and the selection of books every bit as justifiable. Then I could scrap *that* section and do it again. So try as I do to be thoughtful and fair and respectful of authors' work, there's a lot of randomness involved. Write a good book."

Karen Southwick, Editor, Upside Books, Upside Media Inc. (*Upside* magazine)

"Write a good book that stands out from the herd of business management books."

Steve Wasserman, Book Editor, *Los Angeles Times*

"Just write the best book you are capable of writing; then, take solace in the fact that most people do not buy books on the basis of any review they actually read."

Steve's answer to the following question was also insightful: How do you select the books you review?

"With difficulty; 68,000 titles were published in America last year. We have space to attend to about six hundred. I feel much as I imagine a World War I doctor felt on the battlefield of Verdun: it's triage every day."

BOTTOM LINE
THESE RESPONSES SHOW TWO THINGS

1. You must send that news release to the right media for consideration. To send the news release to media who will not be interested is a waste of your time, energy, resources, and money. Targeting the right media is essential.
2. You must create a news release that meets the editorial interest and readership interest of the media you have targeted. It is not hard to garner news coverage if you take your time and do a careful job. The benefits can be phenomenal. You can create news releases that work locally, regionally, or nationally.

When you implement a publicity plan that brings your news to the same media editors repeatedly over time, you can cultivate relationships and become known as a valuable and reliable contributor. And if you give them what their readers want, they give you free publicity.

42

WHERE TO GET E-BOOKS REVIEWED

Every day there are more and more Web sites open for business, so while this list is very extensive it is not complete. Start here but do some searching on your own. All these sites are e-book friendly.

Bella-Online
www.bella-online.net
All genres though favors mainstream and nonfiction.

The Bookdragon Review
www.bookdragonreview.com
All genres of fiction, nonfiction limited to topics on writing.

The BookNook
www.thebooknook.com
All types of electronic books.

Crescent Blues E'Magazine
www.crescentblues.com/3_2issue/homepage.html
Science fiction and mysteries.

eBook Connections
www.ebookconnections.com
All genres.

Fiction Forest
www.fictionforest.com
Fiction.

FOREWORD Magazine
www.forewordmagazine.com
All genres; books must be submitted by the publisher, not the author.

genrEZONE
www.genrezone.com
All genres.

Huntress Book Reviews
www. huntressreviews.com
Fiction.

Inscriptions
www.inscriptionsmagazine.com
Adult fiction and nonfiction.

Just Views
www.justviews.com
All genres.

Midwest Book Review
www.execpc.com/~mbr/bookwatch
All genres; reviews books after publication.

New & Used Books
www.newandusedbooks.com/reviews.cfm
Mostly romance, mystery, and fantasy.

Romance Communications
www.romcom.com
Romance.

Romantic Notions
www.romanticnotions.com
Romance.

The RunningRiver Reader

www.runningriver.com
Fiction and nonfiction.

Scribe & Quill

www.scribequill.com
Fiction and nonfiction; no strong erotica; no strong violence.

Scribes World Reviews

www.scribesworld.com
All genres.

SF Site

www.sfsite.com
Science fiction and fantasy.

Sharpwriter.com

www.sharpwriter.com
All genres.

Under the Covers Book Reviews

www.silcom.com/~manatee/utc.html
All genres.

Word Museum

www.wordmuseum.com
All genres.

Compiled with the help of Jamie Engle, editor of the eBook Connections (*www.ebookconnections.com*) and ePublishing Connections (*www.epublishingconnections.com*) Web sites.

43

GETTING PUBLICITY ON DISCUSSION LISTS

Angela Adair-Hoy

Offering a free chapter to listservs or discussion lists (where people gather online to talk about issues and subjects that matter to them) is an excellent opportunity to get your book mentioned by a list owner!

Tell the list owner that you'd like to offer a free chapter of your book to their readers. You can 1) send the sample chapter to the list owner so they can post it to their discussion list, or 2) offer to let their members e-mail you to request a sample chapter. Provide your Web site's URL in all correspondence so their readers can find more information on your book. What you'll often find is that list owners will just forward your message directly to their list. Since the message comes directly from the list owner, the list members won't accuse you of spamming them.

Or ask the list owner if they will mention your new book's release and provide your Web site's URL for readers to learn more about your book or to download a free chapter.

BE GENEROUS TO LIST OWNERS

Offer a free copy of your entire book or e-book to discussion list owners. If you're marketing a print book only, you might want to consider distributing electronic editions of your book when performing this marketing ploy because of the large number of discussion lists online.

FREE CHAPTER TIPS

Free chapters can be in text, PDF, or HTML format and sent by e-mail, or zipped and located on your Web site's server for download. Not only does this make customer downloads possible, but it also gives the impression that your site is user-friendly, high-tech, and professional. To see how it's done, you can request a free text-only sample chapter by autoresponder at: *www.booklocker.com/authors/hlisle.html*.

When customers download a free chapter, they have the impression that they are receiving a true product. This is important. Posting a free chapter on your Web site does not give this impression, only the impression of reading just another Web page.

DISTRIBUTING FREE CHAPTERS BY E-MAIL

This is a viable alternative for delivery of sample chapters as well as entire e-books that are not too large in size. I frequently distribute e-books as e-mail attachments, but they must be less than one meg in size. You do not want to cause the shutdown of a paying customer's computer!

SAMPLE CHAPTER DELIVERY E-MAIL MESSAGE

FROM: YOU@YOUREMAILADDRESS.COM
TO: YOURREADER@THEIRPLACE.COM
SUBJECT: CHAPTER – YOUR BOOK'S TITLE
PRIORITY: NORMAL

PLEASE FIND ATTACHED:

QTY.: 1

PRODUCT: FREE CHAPTER
YOUR BOOK'S TITLE

NOTE: THIS PRODUCT IS IN PDF FORMAT. IF YOU DO NOT ALREADY HAVE ADOBE ACROBAT READER (IT'S FREE), DOWNLOAD IT HERE AT WWW.ADOBE.COM/PRODINDEX/ACROBAT/READSTEP.HTML-READER

IF YOU DO NOT HAVE THE MOST RECENT VERSION OF THE READER, YOU NEED TO DOWNLOAD IT AT THE URL ABOVE TO READ THIS E-BOOK.

IN THIS MESSAGE, THERE IS A FILE ATTACHMENT FOR THE PRODUCT. CLICK ON IT ONCE AND SAVE IT TO THE FOLDER WHERE YOU SAVE MOST OF YOUR DOCU-MENTS.

THEN, OPEN THE ADOBE ACROBAT READER, CLICK ON FILE, OPEN, AND FIND WHERE YOU SAVED THE PRODUCT.

IF YOU HAVE ANY FUTURE QUESTIONS ABOUT E-BOOKS, PLEASE DON'T HESI-TATE TO CONTACT YOURNAME@YOUREMAILADDRESS.COM.

DISTRIBUTING DOWNLOAD INFORMATION BY E-MAIL

To send your customer download instructions for an e-book they have just purchased, try this:

SAMPLE E-MAIL FOR E-BOOK/CHAPTER DOWNLOAD INSTRUCTIONS

FROM: YOU@YOUREMAILADDRESS.COM
TO: YOURREADER@THEIRPLACE.COM
SUBJECT: DELIVERY: SAMPLE CHAPTER
PRIORITY: NORMAL

THANK YOU FOR ORDERING A SAMPLE CHAPTER FROM [NAME OF YOUR BOOK].

YOU CAN DOWNLOAD YOUR SAMPLE AT:
WWW.YOURWEBSITE.COM/SAMPLEEBOOK.ZIP

THIS ITEM IS ZIPPED. IF YOU ARE A PC USER, YOU WILL NEED WINZIP WHICH IS SHAREWARE AND AVAILABLE FOR DOWNLOAD AT: WWW.WINZIP.COM /DOWNLOAD.HTM

IF YOU ARE A MAC USER, YOU WILL NEED A DECOMPRESSION SOFTWARE PRO-GRAM AS WELL SUCH AS STUFFIT.

EBOOKS ARE IN .PDF FORMAT. IF YOU DO NOT ALREADY HAVE ADOBE ACROBAT READER (IT'S FREE), DOWNLOAD IN HERE: HTTP://WWW.ADOBE.COM/PRODINDEX/ ACROBAT/READSTEP.HTML#READER

IF YOU DO NOT HAVE THE MOST RECENT VERSION OF THE READER, YOU NEED TO DELETE YOUR CURRENT VERSION AND THEN DOWNLOAD THE NEW VERSION AT THE URL ABOVE. IF YOU DON'T DELETE THE OLD VERSION, YOU WILL EXPERIENCE PROBLEMS.

THEN, OPEN ADOBE ACROBAT READER, CLICK ON FILE, OPEN, AND FIND WHERE YOU SAVED THE EBOOK(S) YOU DOWNLOADED ABOVE.

IF YOU HAVE PROBLEMS WITH THIS ITEM, PLEASE CONTACT US AT: YOURNAME@YOUREMAILADDRESS.COM.

THANK YOU.

Most discussion list sites have a search function that you can use to find groups discussing a topic or genre that may relate to your book.

Some services such as eGroups (*www.egroups.com*) will even tell you how many participants belong to a list. If you find a list that has just five or ten participants, skip it and go to the next. When you find a great one, click on the list owner's e-mail link and send them a friendly message about your book.

RESOURCES FOR FINDING DISCUSSION LISTS

Catalist
www.lsoft.com/lists/list_q.html

Educational Listservs
www.sfusd.k12.ca.us/resources/listserv.html

Directory of Scholarly and Professional E-Conferences
n2h2.com/KOVACS

eGroups
www.egroups.com

Internet Scout NEW-LIST
scout.cs.wisc.edu/index.html

OLD-NEW-LIST Archives
listserv.nodak.edu

Liszt
www.liszt.com

PAML (Publicly Accessible Mailing Lists)
www.neosoft.com/cgi-bin/paml_search

Prodigy Mailing Lists
goodstuff.prodigy.com/Mailing_Lists/menu.htm

Topica
www.topica.com

44

ELECTRONIC NEWSLETTER PROMOS

Another highly effective method of promoting books online is to offer sample chapters and copies to publishers and editors of e-mags and e-zines (electronic newsletters).

Find lists of electronic publications online at these sites:

Mining Company Newsletters
community.miningco.com/newsletter/index.htm

John Meer's E-zine List
www.meer.net/~johnl/e-zine-list

Liszt
www.liszt.com

eGroups
www.egroups.com

PAML (Publicly Accessible Mailing Lists)
www.neosoft.com/cgi-bin/paml_search

Prodigy Mailing Lists
goodstuff.prodigy.com/Mailing_Lists/menu.htm

John Labovitz's e-zine-list
www.meer.net/~johnl/e-zine-list

E-zineSeek E-mail Newsletter Directory
ezineseek.com

E-zineDirectory.com—E-mail Newsletter Directory
e-zinedirectory.com

45

ONGOING PUBLICITY CAMPAIGN TACTICS

Angela Adair-Hoy

There are a variety of avenues to explore when marketing your book on-line. Try all of my methods. They work.

PARTICIPATING IN DISCUSSION LISTS AND NEWSGROUPS

Participating in discussions that involve the topic of your book is a highly effective publicity tactic. Don't want thousands of e-mails every single day? To be a passive participant, sign up for the digest versions of these lists. Then, you can spend minimal time on this task. Just review the posts each day and reply to a few that may have relevance to your book or audience.

When participating, don't blatantly promote your book (this is spamming), but do provide the title of your book in your signature at the end of each e-mail along with your contact information. Most e-mail programs allow you to create your signature once and then attach it to each e-mail.

Here's my signature:

FREE E-BOOK FOR WRITERS!
HOW TO BE A FREELANCE WRITER:
INCLUDES 103 PAYING MARKETS!

ANGELA ADAIR-HOY, PUBLISHER
WRITERSWEEKLY.COM
HTTP://WWW.WRITERSWEEKLY.COM

See the previous chapter for resources for finding discussion lists in which you can participate.

RESOURCES FOR FINDING NEWSGROUPS

BIZynet
www.bizynet.com/FAQ-NEWS.HTM

Internet FAQ Archives
www.faqs.org/faqs

Tile.Net
tile.net/news

SuperNews
www.supernews.com

Dejanews
www.dejanews.com/home_ps.html

FREE CLASSIFIEDS

At your favorite search engine, search for "free classifieds." Pick the top five or ten according to their placement in the engine, and post free ads for your book.

Here's a secret I wish I'd known when I started out. Do not post ads for your book on the Internet. They won't work. The market reading your classified ad is too broad. Instead, post ads for your free newsletter or free chapter. Don't forget to include the word *free*. Running ads for your free e-mag will increase the number of your subscribers (everyone loves free stuff), and you'll be able to expose yourself to your new readers frequently . . . instead of the one-time exposure you get with regular classified ads.

COOPERATIVE WEB SITE LINKS

Again, surf to your favorite search engine and enter the keywords that match your book's topic. The Web sites that appear at the top of each one are the ones you want to swap links with. Write to the e-mail contact you find on each Web site, introduce yourself as the author of your book, and ask them if they'd like to swap links or banners with you. You can even offer to list their site as a resource in your book. If you publish an e-mag, offer to run free ads for their site.

Also ask if they'd like a free copy of the book, if their readers would like to receive a free chapter, or if they would like to publish an excerpt from your book on their site.

Find cooperative Web sites using these resources:

MSN Web Communities
communities.msn.com/home

Mining Company
www.miningco.com

Alta Vista
www.altavista.com/cgi-bin/query?pg=aq&what=web

Excite
www.excite.com

HotBot
www.hotbot.com/text/default.asp

Infoseek
infoseek.go.com/find?pg=advanced_www.html@ud9=advanced_www

Yahoo!
search.yahoo.com/search/options

CREATING FREE AND EASY BANNERS

You can create your own free banner in minutes. Using your favorite search engine (yes, I'm starting to sound like a broken record), search for "free banners." Or, surf here: *coder.com/creations/banner/banner-form.pl.cgi.*

MAGAZINES

Offer magazines excerpts of your e-book for reprinting. Target magazines that cover your genre. Don't forget to include your e-mail address and Web site URL in your byline and insist the magazine print these. You can also offer free articles to magazines in exchange for printing your byline. Some magazines will pay for your article and also run your byline. Ask the editor if they run bylines before offering to write for free.

46

ADVERTISING: WHERE TO SPEND THAT SPARE CHANGE

M. J. Rose

Contrary to public opinion, not all advertising is cost prohibitive. The key is to figure out who your target audience is and make sure your message is unique, and to the point. The prevailing wisdom is that it takes seven times for an impression to get through to your audience.

So if you are going to buy advertising, make sure you buy multiple ads (at least three). Put your title in the ad at least three times and, if you can, get your book's cover in there, too.

On the following page is a sample ad for *Lip Service*. It ran in one magazine three times and it paid for itself three times over.

It's imperative to make sure that your ad is going to your target audience that we discussed in Chapter One. Don't buy an ad before talking to the sales department of the magazine or e-zine you are considering.

Ask for:

- Sample ads
- A list of advertisers
- Percentage of men vs. women readers
- Average age of audience
- Average income of audience
- Level of education
- Buying habits
- Circulation (if it's a print publication)
- Web site visitors, not impressions (the number of times an ad appears to a visitor on the site) if it's online

Can an erotic book be intelligent?

Lip Service

a novel by M. J. Rose

Yes.

At once a sophisticated love story and a psychological thriller, <u>Lip Service</u> is both seductive and sinister. M. J. Rose has crafted an uninhibited narrative that builds to a shocking crescendo.

Not since Erica Jong's <u>Fear of Flying</u> has a novel so successfully examined the relationship between sexuality and identity.

"<u>Lip Service</u> is erotic. So much so that during my course of reading, my husband was a very happy man. An extremely happy man.

The main character, Julia Sterling, is as strong a female character as you will find in fiction today. She becomes even more so as the story progresses.

I do not want to give away plot. <u>Lip Service</u> should be savored bit by bit. As if unwrapping a special gourmet chocolate treat. Because treat it is indeed. And I, for one, will be savoring the memory of it for a long time to come."

—*Buzz Review News*

"Take a novel in the style of Danielle Steel. Improve the writing by making it a tighter story with believable characters and more substance. Add a sexual theme as well as a heroine capable of saying a bunch of words Steel's characters probably don't even know, and you get the drift of <u>Lip Service</u>, a stylish first novel by M. J. Rose."

—*January Magazine*

Order online at Amazon.com or BarnesandNoble.com or call 800-431-1579. All credit cards accepted.

It's amazing how many online publications will work with you to create targeted campaigns. Don't be shy about calling up or e-mailing and asking for special rates. I've found that many sites were willing to give me a reduced rate because I was an individual rather than a big company.

People are still people and the media salesperson you're talking to on the other end of the phone can get really excited about your project and want to see your advertising there.

Most larger sites will not only help you design a banner (for a fee) but they will custom-build a campaign that shows up only in certain sections of the site. For instance, your banner will only appear on the book page, or the health page.

Smaller sites will exchange content for advertising. I give them an article; they give me banner space for six weeks. Bartering is alive and well on the Web.

One important rule of thumb is that advertising works best when the same ad or banner is seen at least seven times by the viewer. Many advertising gurus claim that it takes those seven impressions before your title or your name will be recognized.

That means that if you can't afford to run the ad at least that many times, don't waste your money.

47

CHEAP ADVERTISING!

Allene Frances

Just Views

justviews.virtualave.net

Accepts ads and trades ads with authors. Although most of the ad space on the review/interview pages will be paid ads, the owner will gladly swap if someone is interested. Send your e-mail request to *justviews@webcombo.net*.

The Celebrity Café

thecelebritycafe.com/advertising.html

Contact: Jean Marie Ward, Editor

Advertising is based on the standard CPM impression type. (CPM, or Clicks Per Mile, means "cost per thousand." For example, a $50 CPM means that for every 1000 times you show an ad, it costs the advertiser $50. So, if you sell a $10/CPM ad, and your e-mag goes out to 15,000 subscribers, the advertiser will pay you $150, or $10 x 15.) CPM usually goes for anywhere between $15 and $25. The magazine has been in existence for over two years now and also sells five-line ads in their newsletter at a fixed rate of $10 per 1,000 newsletter readers (which totals $200 at their current circulation).

Crescent Blues

www.crescentblues.com

Standard banner: $125/month

Standard thumbnail posted on left navigation bar of all pages: $30/month

Word Museum

www.wordmuseum.com
P.O. Box 452, Greenfield, IN 46140
Contact: Lori Soard
Phone: 317-462-0037
E-mail: *wordmuseum@wordmuseum.com*
Circulation of *Yellow Sticky Notes:* 2,000
Word Museum publishes *Wordbeats* (a weekly newsletter) and *Yellow Sticky Notes* (semiannual). Ads in *Wordbeats* are fee to authors or $5 per issue for commercial advertisers. Ads in *Yellow Sticky Notes* are $20 for a quarter page, $50 for a half page, $60 for a full page.

Inscriptions

www.incriptionsmagazine.com
432 S. B Street, Lake Worth, FL 33460
Contact: Jade Walker, Editor
Phone: 561-533-5844
Fax: 815-346-1770
E-mail: *editor@inscriptionsmagazine.com*
Circulation of e-zine: 2,600
Runs free ads for authors who submit acceptable articles to appear in their e-zine, *Inscriptions,* which has a circulation of 2,600, targeting professional working writers, editors, and publishers. E-zine ads (to 50 words) are $5 per issue ($25 for six weeks). Banner ad on Web site is $25/issue ($125 for six weeks). They will also design your banner for only $50. Also sells combination e-zine/banner ad packages.

ForeWord Magazine

www.forewordmagazine.com
129 ½ E. Front Street, Traverse City, MI 49684
Contact: Victoria Sutherland
Phone: 231-933-3699
E-mail: *victoria@foreowordmagazine.com*
Circulation: 15,000
Provides booksellers, librarians, and publishing professionals with a monthly source of news and reviews covering the vital arm of the publishing trade—the independent and university press industry. Readers are booksellers and librarians whose primary function is buying responsibility for

their bookstore/library. Black-and-white print ad rates range from $310 to $1,850 depending on size.

Romantic Notions

romanticnotions.com
P.O. Box 705, Salem, OR 97308
Contact: Michelle Marr
Phone: 503-589-0476
E-mail: *michelle@romanticnotions.com*

Occasionally swaps ad space for services of freelance writers. Rates vary. "Our sites do not accept paid advertising from individual romance authors, but we offer free banner space and other promotional opportunities." See *romanticnotions.com/promotion.html* for details.

WritersWeekly.com

www.writersweekly.com/index-advertise.htm
Circulation: 40,000+

Rates appear at Web site. Doug Clegg, author of the world's first sponsored e-serial, ran an ad in *Writers Weekly* seeking new subscribers for his new, free e-serial. He then wrote, saying, "The response from your list was overwhelming—definitely made the cost of the ad seem puny. I think this was the most cost-effective ad I've ever taken on the Internet."

ANOTHER RESOURCE FOR CHEAP ADVERTISING

E-Mail Newsletters and E-Zines That Accept Advertising and Sponsorships

www.copywriter.com/lists/ezines.htm

Allene Frances is an e-book author and owner of the online bookstore Books from the Heart (*www.booksfromtheheart.net*). Visit her author page at *allenefrances.virtualave.net*.

48

FREE, FREE, FREE

M. J. Rose

The most potent word to anyone involved with promotion and publicity is only four letters long. Not to be repetitive, but the word is "Free."

Just stop and think for a minute how many offers you see from brand name products and services that include a free offer.

Banks offer free checking with deposits. Cosmetic companies offer free samples. Car companies offer free CD players during big promos. The concept of "free" is an important part of many marketing strategies.

And nothing is easier or less expensive for an author of an e-book or a print book that can be sent out via electronic download than to offer free books. Before we discuss why you should give out free books, let's look at one of the basic precepts of marketing.

In order for your name or the name of your book to sink into the reader's mind it has to have been seen about seven times. Twenty years ago it only took three times to get name recognition for a person or product, but there is so much more advertising now that the number's gone up.

But it's not easy to get that kind of mention. So I believe we have to use other tools at our disposal. And one of the best I know is giving your book away for free for a certain amount of time.

FACING FACTS

Making a huge profit is not most authors' motivation. Except for the best-selling authors, few of us can afford to write full-time without taking on other jobs. So giving away a few hundred or a few thousand copies of your book probably won't change your lifestyle. If you are like me, I never even thought I'd break even on my book-publishing venture.

But one thing I will promise you is that every free book you give away will be more valuable to you than the few dollars you might have made on it.

CASE HISTORIES

Seth Godin

Seth Godin, a *New York Times* best-selling business author (*Permission Marketing*) recently offered his new book—*Unleashing the Idea Virus*—as a free e-book to everyone who wanted it. He did not expect to make a dime on the e-book itself.

His plan was to use the free offer to get people talking about the book. (Here *we* are talking about it, right?) His plan was to offer the e-book free at *www.ideavirus.com* and then five months later sell a hardcover version.

When I interviewed him about why he was making this radical offer he told me that there are so many books out there that if we expect people to find our books—let alone buy them—we have nothing but an uphill battle before us.

Godin's idea is that if he gives the book away he can make money other ways. One is speaking on the lecture circuit about why he gave his book away. Another is writing about his experience for magazines that will pay him. And a third is that enough people will start to read his book as an e-book and then realize they like it and want to own a print copy.

Well, it worked. He got press in Wirednews.com, *USA Today, Fast Company* magazine, and a host of others.

Douglas Clegg

Douglas Clegg, a contributor to this book, has been giving away free serialized versions of his books via e-mail for over two years. He reports that it has built up his audience to the point that he was able to sell the print rights of those same books for more than he'd ever previously received from a publisher.

Anne Rice

Anne Rice and her publisher recently sold Contentville.com (*www. contentville.com*) the rights to post two free chapters of her newest novel online. Now, granted two chapters are not a free book, but Contentville. com did pay Rice a four-figure sum to post those chapters. However Rice is already a household name. What's important about this is that despite how successful she is and how many millions of books she sells, her publishing house understands the concept of *free*.

Stephen King

We can't discuss free books without talking about Stephen King. When his first e-book was released, Amazon.com and Barnes & Noble paid King's publisher for each copy but then offered the book free to the public. Over a half a million people downloaded that free e-book within the first forty-eight hours.

Overnight, people who had never heard about e-books knew what they were.

On the other hand, when King offered his first serial on the Web (*www. stephenking.com*) and charged one dollar for the first chapter, only 140,000 downloaded it. While I would be delighted with those numbers, the point is that over three times more people downloaded the free book.

John Sedgwick

The protagonist in John Sedgwick's debut novel, *The Dark House* (Harper-Collins), follows strangers in their cars. So, Sedgwick, a journalist who writes for publications like *GQ, Atlantic Monthly,* and *Worth,* penned *The Stalker's Diary*—a free five-part series. The idea was to give the series away in an effort to attract readers to his novel. The diary entries recounted how Sedgwick decided to imitate his main character by stalking people in his own car. Then, working with his editor Sedgwick proposed the promotion to barnes&noble.com. It was the biggest promotion bn.com had ever done for a first novelist, according to Andy LeCount, features editor at bn.com.

And it worked. Response in terms of book sales was significant.

SHOULD YOU GIVE AWAY THE WHOLE BOOK?

Not necessarily. Many authors give away free chapters to their new work. But consider what you have to gain or lose by giving away the first 1,000 copies. If you are netting $3 per copy of your e-book you would lose your first $3,000.

What are you gaining? Let's start locally.

You most probably can get press from your local newspaper, TV station, or radio station.

Chances are one newspaper story and one radio mention would reach at least 100,000 potential readers and listeners. There is no way you could buy that kind of notice with the $3,000 you might have gotten in sales. There is no way you could buy that kind of notice with $5,000. And don't forget, press coverage—editorial content—pulls more weight than ads.

Consumers aren't stupid. They know the advertiser pays for ads. And they also know you cannot buy your way into print. (Well, some people can, but that's another subject for another book.) If you promote the give-away correctly on the Web and go after at least two or three big sites, there's no question you can get coverage from sites that have some connection to the theme of your book and reach at least another 200,000 people.

So now 300,000 people have heard about your book. If just one percent goes to your site to get the free copy—3,000 people will show up at your site.

The first 1,000 will get the book. The next 2,000 might buy the book. But certainly they are a captive audience on your site and if your site has a free excerpt for the losers and some interesting graphics and engaging copy—you might sell the book to many of them.

But 300,000 people have heard or read about your book. And 1,000 have gotten a copy for free. So you now have people talking about you. And it didn't actually cost you a dime.

Don't forget that if half of the people who download the book for free like it, and each one tells ten people, then 5,000 more people will hear about the book. And if each one of those people tells another ten people . . . well, you get the idea.

49

E-MAIL PROMOTION TACTICS

Greg Mitchell

I knew something was happening when I got a note from a woman in Oklahoma who said she had just ordered six copies of my book for all the fathers she knew who "needed" it. On the same day in April, I received another e-mail from a man in North Carolina who wanted to send me pictures of the full-scale Little League field he had built in his backyard. He wanted me to forward the photos to Hollywood in case someone was scouting around for locations for a movie based on the book.

I got a million of 'em. Well, maybe not a million, but an overstuffed e-mail box full of notes from people (actual or potential readers) across the country in response to my personal e-mail blitz promoting my latest book. The letters are still pouring in as I write this, and I'm ready to declare it a tremendous success already.

As usual, the best ideas are born of desperation.

I've been involved with self-promoting my books for nearly twenty years. But, needless to say, times and opportunities have changed. My new book is my sixth, but only the second since the Internet really took off.

My previous books were all in the serious, midlist nonfiction vein—political, topical, or historical—and published by major houses such as Random House, Putnam, and Viking. Although I received what most authors would probably feel was ample publicity support, I never felt that it was enough (naturally) and always took a strong role in helping the cause via phone calls, letters, arm-twisting, and articles. Publicists tended to love me (when I wasn't meddling too much) because I did a pretty terrific job at this, and they could claim partial (or full) credit. My books tended to have a much higher profile than seemed "natural," even though they were well reviewed and received awards and award nominations (all of which did not boost sales much). I mean, I've been on *The Today Show, Larry King, Charlie Rose,* and *Entertainment Tonight.*

My latest book, however, is quite a departure: a memoir of one season coaching my son in Little League, called *Joy in Mudville.* Some of my old rules for promotion would no longer apply because of the subject matter. It was not likely to automatically receive major reviews, for example.

Ironically, *Joy in Mudville* seemed to me to have the best commercial potential of any of my books. It was funny, not serious, and dealt with family issues of possible interest to all parents, while at the same time appealing to an ever-wider baseball audience. It had already been optioned for a movie by Universal Pictures, at the behest of Tom Hanks.

My agent, my former editor, and other writers all advised me to hire an outside publicist. But the book was already in the stores, and most of the freelance publicists felt it was "too late already." (This you don't want to hear.) Then there is the cost—in the thousands and tens of thousands.

So I decided to "take it to the streets"—or the grassroots, as it were, since we're talking baseball here. With previous books, I'd always fantasized about reaching the most likely potential readers directly. Like most authors, I figured that if I could just get a notice or letter in the hands of, say, 50,000 people in the prime audience for the book, I could sell 10,000 copies right there. But who could locate these people and afford to print and mail that many letters?

If you use AOL you can search the member directory, typing in words related to your book, which pulls up matches in "profiles" supplied by many users to the service. This will get you one hundred suitable e-mail addresses at a pop. A word of warning, however: AOL's terms of service forbid you from searching the directory for commercial purposes or sending fellow members "solicitations." There may be a gray area, however, if you just send off a friendly note expressing your shared interests, or perhaps mentioning your book in passing or in your e-mail's signature.

Still, even if you use AOL this way, the number of contacts they will provide is limited. And a couple of hundred fanatics, even if they bought a book for themselves and their therapist, would not really make a deep impact in your book sales. So I looked to the Web beyond AOL as my happy hunting ground.

But how to identify a much wider audience?

Well, there are many baseball sites on the Net. Probably too many. This may be true in your interest area, as well. The biggest site I could make use of, I knew, was Skilton's Links, which lists over 6,500 baseball sites broken into more than a dozen categories, with subcategories under that. No way I could reach all 6,500, nor would I want to, as most are simply shrines for star players or favorite teams or fantasy baseball stat services. While I might find some readers there, the percentage would likely be fairly low. As Tug McGraw (Tim's Dad) once said, "Ya gotta believe"—in sifting and sorting.

I settled on two main links areas—one for coaches (mainly instructional stuff) and another for youth leagues (mainly league or team sites). First, I hit the coaches with the brief e-mail notice about my book. I wanted them as readers, of course, but they could do so much more for me: for example, sell my book on their sites, review or endorse the book, or put up an excerpt from the book or an article I'd written derived from it. I hit about one hundred such sites and got a tremendous response: more than a few sales, and several put the book up for sale (or blurbed it and linked it to Amazon.com), or offered to run my pieces. If I did nothing else, that alone would extend my reach to a core audience quite a bit.

But I went further—much further. I started contacting some of the thousands of youth leagues listed at Skilton, starting with A for Alabama. I found, upon reaching a few sites, that there was always at least one key person I could e-mail in a flash, just clicking on the blue underlined contact person or the "e-mail us" person. Poking around a little deeper (the way I've done in library stacks), I might find the league's entire board of directors, with most of them underlined in blue for quick service. This was heaven. A few leagues went so far as to put up e-mail addresses for a dozen or more of my fellow coaches—my absolute target audience! Talk about nirvana. In a matter of minutes I could pass along to thirty or more core readers, directly, and at no real cost, some tasteful hype for my book.

Indeed, my goal was to be as soft a sell as possible. In two short paragraphs I briefly described the book and very casually mentioned that they could read much more about it at Amazon.com (where I knew the very positive early reviews and customer comments had been posted). The messages were largely boilerplate, if folksy, though I sometimes inserted a reference to their home state. Beyond that I did not make a sales pitch—if they went to Amazon they would already be in the store—and of course wished them a great season, from one coach to another.

Immediately, I got a few letters of interest and support and only one note complaining about being targeted that way. Two weeks later, as I continued the campaign, I had a couple more reviews to tout (including *USA Today* and *Baseball America*).

Realizing that it would take weeks to get through all fifty states part-time, I asked my sister-in-law to lend support. Over the next two weeks, she and I together sent out roughly two thousand e-mails. We continued to get a heartfelt and enthusiastic response, from men and women, with replies testifying to their own Little League passion—and problems—or at the least congratulations on writing a "much-needed" book and promises to check it out (or, even, claims to having just ordered it online). A week later some wrote again to say they had already read the book and loved it.

Again, no more than one or two responded by complaining that they'd been "spammed." I figured that nearly everyone felt happy to be treated like an elite member of this special baseball club (or cult). I believe that people who are genuinely involved in specific interests do not mind getting e-mails in those areas.

As I write this, it is too early to recognize the ripple effect, but I sense from the Amazon rankings that we have found a steady line of purchasers that I could only attribute to the e-mail campaign.

Greg Mitchell's other books include *Tricky Dick and the Pink Lady: Richard Nixon vs. Helen Gahagan Douglas; The Campaign of the Century: Upton Sinclair's Race for Governor of California* (both Random House); and *Hiroshima in America,* with Robert Jay Lifton (Putnam). His next book is another collaboration with Lifton, *Who Owns Death: Capital Punishment, The American Conscience and the End of Executions* (William Morrow).

50

E-SERIALS!

Douglas Clegg

Each year, I write a novel and give it away to readers, one chapter at a time, by e-mail . . . free. This year, three companies bid for sponsorship of my new e-serial novel that was set to launch in late July. I'd only written one short chapter, and three companies were offering money to be able to grab sponsorship of something that would not happen for months.

The winner came up with a nice amount for me—simply for the rights to sponsor my e-mail list. I retained hard/soft print rights on the book itself.

The e-serial in question, *Nightmare House,* is my second e-serial. *Publishers Weekly* called my first e-mail novel, *Naomi,* "the first major work of fiction to originate in cyberspace." (Of course, there wasn't much fiction published in cyberspace then.)

You might ask how could you write a novel and then hand it over to a reader for nothing? But you must remember that someone is paying you to do this. Paying you a good amount of money! As much as you could get if you went to a big publisher and were paid a nice advance—maybe more if you're good at setting your fee.

Sounds a little like the other broadcast media—radio and television, right?

Well, that's where I got the idea. It seemed natural to me that people might be more willing to read a book online if they didn't have to pay for it. And just as detergent manufacturers and candy makers advertise on television by sponsoring a television show, why not find a company to sponsor my book?

E-mail was the natural form of distribution because everyone on the Internet has an e-mail account. The serial form seemed a natural, too. Charles Dickens wrote much of his fiction for serial publication; Tom Wolfe wrote the original draft of *Bonfire of the Vanities* in serial form for *Rolling Stone* magazine; and both Stephen King and John Saul wrote serial installments of their novels, *The Green Mile* and *The Blackstone Chronicles.* I loved the form because there was always the suspense of wondering, what would happen next?

As it turns out, various writers had been trying out serial fiction in e-mail already, but none of them had found a way to get paid for their efforts and still offer their fiction free to readers. I think writers should always get paid.

So, I became "the first novelist to create the world's first sponsored e-mail serial novel." I know it's a mouthful. I try not to say it too often or take it too seriously.

Here's the thing: I've written several novels that have come out in paperback and hardcover from various publishers: Pocket, Dell, Leisure, Kensington, Cemetery Dance, Subterranean Press, and others. But when I decided to write a novel entirely in e-mail for serial installments, I wanted to take it further and offer it free to readers. So I did—and still got paid for it. Then I sold the hardcover and paperback rights . . . without an agent.

I made more on that one book than I had for my previous paperback. How'd this happen?

First, I've noticed that if you really want to do something that sounds good, there are ways to figure it out. Ways that are joyful, healthy, and legal—for those of you who might be criminally inclined.

Second, I set up a Web site and got the word around the Internet that I was doing this. Since I write horror fiction, I approached primarily horror Web sites, e-zines, and discussion lists to help get the word out. Find the community online most receptive to your kind of fiction, and enlist their help and expertise. What makes the Internet work, in my opinion, is the sense of community that develops between people of like minds.

The next step was to create a list called the DouglasClegg list at what is now eGroups.com, a free service and very supportive. Suddenly, *Publishers Weekly, Business Week, Business 2.0, Time,* and many other magazines and newspapers were calling me to find out just what this was. This exploded the word about the e-serial, which made it fun and newsworthy.

If you're going to do this, be sure and announce it to the world at least six months ahead of time. Don't announce it and then start the novel the following month. You need to allow time for people to hear about it and sign up for it. For my first e-serial novel, *Naomi,* I had people from India,

Italy, Greece, and England sign up—as well as many from the U.S. and Australia. For all I know, people from other countries also were on the list. It takes time for word on a project like this to travel the globe. Give it time— and let your imagination percolate for your novel in the meantime.

From there, I wrote the novel, week by week, and sent out the chapters by e-mail—about 3,000 words per week for several months. I'm a disciplined writer. I know I can write each week what I set out to write. I'm also lazy in all other disciplines, which helps. The novelist Sloan Wilson once wrote something to the effect that "the grass will grow long" if one intends to write a novel. Let the grass grow long. Write the novel.

Now, you can write the entire novel ahead of time if you're insecure about being able to produce on a schedule. I wanted to make the novel as fun for me as for readers, so I enjoyed that extra adrenaline rush of writing the novel week-by-week. One weekend in July during the writing of *Naomi,* I attended a convention called Necon—and just went into my room, away from the crowd, to write the installment of the novel due to my readers that weekend. The more time pressure on my imagination, the better the story comes through. I would not expect every writer to be as quirky about this as I am.

But wait. You want to know how I went about getting sponsorships, right?

All right, first I followed what's considered a basic notion of investing: Find out what you yourself already know about and like, and invest in that. I had a preexisting relationship with my publisher, Dorchester Publishing (my paperbacks were being published by their Leisure Books imprint). I love this company. They're practically like family to me. I had been approached by one company on the Internet already, but the company had no connection to books or readers, so I didn't think it would be a good fit. I mentioned to my publisher that I was looking for a sponsor. They jumped at the chance.

This was great. They actually came up with a little more money than I was going to ask for, and I was able to use this money to pay for banner ads for the e-serial, and to pay a friend who had put together the first version of my Web site and helped me with promotion.

Around Christmas of that year, when I knew what my next e-serial would be, I sent out a note to my list, mentioning that I was looking for a sponsor for the new, upcoming e-mail novel. I was pleasantly shocked to find that three different companies were interested. Now, I'm not the greatest businessman in the world, and I liked each of the people who approached me. So I told each of them by Friday night of that week that I'd had other interest, so they needed to put their most aggressive bids in. They did. By Monday morning, the winner was Cemetery Dance Publications. Cemetery Dance (also known as CD) is one of the premier deluxe limited edition publishers. I had already built a business relationship with them, so this was not going too far afield. And I love the books they publish, which include some of my favorite authors, including Dean Koontz, Richard Laymon, and others.

One piece of advice I'd give those looking for sponsorships: Your best bet is going to be a company that is somehow closely married to the kind of readers your novel will attract.

So far, I've stuck with publishers as sponsors because these are the people I've worked with, whom I trust, who trust me, and who are most likely to want to reach horror fiction readers with their sponsorship. However, let your mind roam when coming up with sponsors: after all, what if I got the Jaycees, who annually sponsor haunted houses around the country, to sponsor a special October horror e-serial? How about a site like Horror-Online.com, which is run by Universal Studios? When Wes Craven has a new horror movie coming out, his studio could sponsor horror fiction on the Internet in order to get the buzz going early about the upcoming frightfest in the theaters. There are a lot of possibilities.

After having written *Naomi,* with the onslaught of news stories that were generated from this, I was amazed to see how many new, highly publicized serials were debuting on the Internet. New names in fiction, as well as names that had erupted in the digital world of fiction from the late 1990s (Richard Wright, Charlotte Boyett-Compo, Steve Savile, Steven Lee Climer, Brian Hopkins, and many others).

iUniverse.com, in conjunction with Random House, serialized Mark Danielewski's *House of Leaves* on their site. Even Stephen King decided to do an e-serial called *The Plant* after the phenomenal—but not unexpected—success of his entry into e-books with the novella *Riding the Bullet,* published in March 2000. MightyWords.com sells serialized material. So the serial is back with the Internet, and I'm glad I got into it early, at least in Internet-time, which is the day before yesterday. I also hope other writers will embrace this form. There's a place in our culture for every kind of book now, thanks to the digital world.

For more information about Douglas Clegg's current or upcoming e-serial novels, e-mail *dclegg@douglasclegg.com* with "subscribe" in the subject line of your e-mail.

51

E-MAGS: THE SUPREME MARKETING TOOL FOR YOUR BOOK

Angela Adair-Hoy

Imagine being able to place free ads in a magazine that has thousands of subscribers who are specifically interested in reading about the topic of your book on a weekly or monthly basis. Imagine being able to run unlimited ads for your book targeting this highly effective and *buying* list of subscribers. Imagine . . . owning your own magazine and doing whatever the heck you want for shameless self-promotion!

An e-mag (aka electronic magazine, e-zine, or electronic newsletter) is an electronic publication delivered by e-mail to paying or nonpaying subscribers. E-mags can be sent in the body of an e-mail or as an e-mail attachment.

A consumer must see your ad many times to respond. If you publish an e-mag, your readers will see your ad on a regular basis. Will sales increase? You bet they will!

My e-mag, *WritersWeekly,* is distributed to more than 40,000 writers every Wednesday. Total readership exceeds 50,000. I place advertisements for my own products in each issue that generate thousands of dollars in sales every week.

IN THE BEGINNING . . .

In June 1997, the first issue of *The Write Markets Report* hit the printing press. I tend to do things quickly and . . . without thinking. Only one month after the magazine idea hit me, the first issue was complete. I began selling the print magazine for $39 per year (12 issues). I was doing all the work, including interviewing editors, writing, hiring freelancers, processing subscriptions, maintaining the subscriber database and the accounting software . . . all without too much trouble.

In early 1998, I wrote, formatted, and printed my first book, *How to Be a Syndicated Newspaper Columnist*. I began selling the book accompanied by a disk of 6,000+ newspaper markets. I ran ads for my own book in *The Write Markets Report*. My subscribers knew I provided a quality magazine, so they trusted me to provide a quality book as well. The book sold very well at $14.95 per copy.

Then, another idea hit me. What if I offered a free, abbreviated electronic sample (teaser issue) of my magazine each month? I could build a new subscriber database for that one and readers would see my ads over and over again. It would be free, so thousands would sign up. Hey! I was onto something here!

I quickly formatted the first issue of *National Writer's Monthly* (now called *WritersWeekly.com*). I included quality market information along with plenty of ads for my products. Sales increased and so did the number of subscribers. The more subscribers I attracted to the free e-mag, the more sales I processed. And, pretty soon, I had enough subscribers to be attractive to advertisers.

TOPIC

Be sure the primary topic of your e-mag complements your book and provides plenty of ideas for secondary products you can produce and sell. If there is nothing else you can sell to your readers, then your e-mag will not be profitable. For example, I sell e-books and media directories for writers and sponsor a profitable quarterly twenty-four-hour short story contest.

Remember, your e-mag will be your selling vehicle for all future products. Another hint is to write your future books on topics that target your already existing audience. With each new book I self-publish, my income increases.

FORMAT

You are welcome to use my e-mag's format in making your first newsletter. Receive the current issue within seconds by sending any e-mail to *webmaster @writersweekly.com*. Then delete my editorial material and write your own.

CONTENT

The secret to getting and keeping subscribers is to provide quality editorial content. My e-mag originally featured a Q&A column, online resources for writers, and paying markets. However, I listened to my readers to find out what they really needed. I now feature current freelance job listings and paying markets. My new column, "The Publisher's Desk," has become a consumer advocate forum for writers. We run letters from writers alerting us to unscrupulous firms and greedy publishing contracts. We have successfully caused contractual changes benefiting freelance writers and self-published authors. I'm quite sure that the controversial nature of the column keeps readers coming back for more, week after week. But I also receive dozens of letters every week from writers who have landed freelance jobs and assignments through my listings. This type of quality editorial content continues to increase my circulation, advertising income, and sales.

I highly recommend starting an e-mag on the topic or genre of your book and distributing it free of charge. For step-by-step instructions, consider reading my book, *Profitable E-mail Publishing: How to Publish a Profitable E-mag*. For the table of contents and an excerpt, see *www.writersweekly.com/index-ezines.htm*.

OUTSTANDING RESOURCES FOR E-MAG PUBLISHERS

Free Articles to Publish in Your E-mag

IdeaMarketers
www.ideamarketers.com

Traffic Central
www.trafficcentral.net/articles.htm

Writers & Publishers Connection

E-mail your subscription request to: *writers98@aol.com*

Where to Register Your E-Mag

The Internet Scout NEW-LIST Mailing List
(I give this one five stars!)

scout.cs.wisc.edu/index.html

E-ZINESearch

homeincome.com/search-it/ezine

The List of Lists

catalog.com/vivian/interest-group-search.html

You Must Subscribe to This!

E-zine-Tips

ezine-tips.com

A free daily e-zine offering tips, reviews, and resources to help you produce, grow, and manage a quality e-zine

To join, e-mail: *join-e-zine-tips@sparklist.com*

52

SECRETS OF CREATING AND MAINTAINING A SUCCESSFUL E-ZINE

Debbie Ridpath Ohi

When I first began *Inkspot* in 1995, it was one of the only e-zines for writers on the Web. It began as a hobby, funded out of my own pocket and maintained in my spare time. *Inkspot* is now my full-time career.

I have no marketing or publishing background, and I took no courses in HTML; I learned everything through trial and error as well as a great deal of online research. Here are a few tips I've learned about creating and maintaining a successful e-zine:

CHOOSE YOUR NICHE

Do a lot of research before you launch your e-zine. Analyze your competition. If you discover that there are already dozens of e-zines very similar to the one you plan to launch, you may want to consider narrowing its focus. Offer potential readers something they can't find anywhere else.

MAKE A BUSINESS PLAN

I wish I had done this from the beginning. After you figure out what kind of e-zine you plan to create, ask yourself how much time and money you want to invest. Who will your target audience be? How do you plan on attracting subscribers? Will you make money through subscription fees or advertising revenue? What are your goals?

UPDATE FREQUENTLY AND CONSISTENTLY

This is absolutely essential. It will do you no good to invest time and money in an impressive launch if you don't plan to commit to the project long-term. Establish a realistic update or publication schedule and stick to it. Readers will quickly lose interest in a stale e-zine.

BE A FILTER

Be an information filter. The Internet is no longer a novelty, and its vast wealth of available information can be overwhelming to the casual user. Make sure your content is carefully researched, proofread, and edited. Verify your sources. Minimize the noise factor.

KNOW YOUR AUDIENCE

Encourage reader feedback. Send out surveys. Find out what your readers like and don't like. Learn how to gauge reader response.

MAKE SURE YOUR E-ZINE IS READABLE

Format your e-zine so that everyone can easily read it. If you are sending out an e-mail newsletter, for example, avoid fancy styles and "curly quotes." If your e-zine is Web-based and relies heavily on graphics, remember that some users may be using slow connections or looking at your e-zine with their graphics option turned off on their browsers.

PROMOTE, PROMOTE, PROMOTE!

Be active in promoting your e-zine, especially online. Use e-mail, newsgroups, search engines, e-zine directories, your signature, message boards and mailing lists, strategic links, chats . . . but learn how to do it without spamming. Establish yourself as an expert on your topic. Get yourself interviewed. Get people to write about you and your e-zine.

NETWORK

Get to know the other people in the business. Be friendly. I've found that a cooperative approach tends to work much better than an aggressive one on the Internet.

Good luck!

Debbie Ridpath Ohi is the publisher and editor of *Inkspot* (*www.inkspot.com*), a free award-winning Web resource and community for writers. Debbie's book, *The Writer's Online Marketplace,* is available from *Writer's Digest* Books.

53

REGISTERING WITH SEARCH ENGINES

Angela Adair-Hoy

Have you ever wondered how people register their sites with all the search engines? We're sharing our secret way with you . . . but it is time consuming.

If you want someone else to do the legwork, you can't beat the results of SubmitPlus. We highly recommend signing up for their "Top 40 Positions" program for $139. See *submitplus.bc.ca*.

If you'd like to save a few bucks, you can register your book's Web page with the major search engines all by yourself. This process may take a couple of days to complete. But, the rewards will be wonderful! What you'll be doing is promoting your book online by posting your book's Web page to a variety of search engines, FAQ sites, and other sites as well. This form makes it easy to do, and it's (almost) fun!

Type the information from the following section into a word processing or text document. This will make it easy to cut and paste the information while you're registering your book's Web page with the engines. Some search engines request all of these items, while others only request some of them.

INFORMATION THE SEARCH ENGINES NEED

Your Book Page's URL: for example: *www.yourbooktitle.com*
Contact Name: your name
Contact E-mail: you@yourisp.com

Contact Phone: your-phone-number
Contact Fax: your-fax-number

Note: If you don't have a fax number, you can obtain a free one at Efax.com (*www.efax.com*). Faxes sent to your fax number are then e-mailed to you.

Name: The name of your company or your name
Address: Your complete address
URL: The URL where people can read about and order your book
Description: Three descriptive sentences about your book
Keywords:

Note: Some sites only let you type in ten descriptive words. Others let you type in 50. Complete all of these. Place your key words in order from most important to least important.

10 words: ten, key, words, about, your, book, separated, by, commas
20 words: copy, the, ten, above, and, add, ten, more
50 words: copy, the, twenty, above, and, add, thirty, more

ENGINES WHERE YOU CAN REGISTER

Now, using the information above, go to each of these search engines and start registering your book page there.

Alta Vista
altavista.digital.com/cgi-bin/query?pg=addurl

Ask Jeeves
www.askjeeves.com
Must send e-mail to request they include your Web site to: *url@askjeeves.com*

Excite
www.excite.com/Info/add_url.html

GO Network
www.go.com/AddUrl?pg=SubmitUrl.html

Google
www.google.com

Hotbot
www.hotbot.com/addurl.html

Infoseek
infoseek.go.com/AddUrl?pg=SubmitUrl.html

Lycos
www.lycos.com/addasite.html

MSN
search.msn.com/addurl.asp

Northern Light
www.northernlight.com/docs/register.htm

SearchKing
www.searchking.com/add_url.htm

REX
www.rex-search.com/add

Webcrawler
www.webcrawler.com/WebCrawler/SubmitURLS.html

GENERAL DIRECTORIES

HandiLinks
www.handilinks.com/addform.htm

InfoMine
infomine.ucr.edu/participants/netgain.html

Jayde
www.jayde.com/cgi-bin/addurl.cgi

JumpCity
www.jumpcity.com/send-page.html

LinkCentre
linkcentre.com/addurl.html

Nerd World Media
www.nerdworld.com/cgi-bin/nwadd.cgi

OneKey
www.onekey.com/live/addurl.htm

Scrub the Web
www.scrubtheweb.com/addurl.html

Snap!
www.snap.com
(Must select category)

Starting Point
www.stpt.com/submit/submit.asp

Turnpike Emporium
www.turnpike.net/directory.html?getentry

What's New
www.whatsnu.com/add.html

What's New Too!
newtoo.manifest.com/submit.html

Yahoo!
www.yahoo.com

INDUSTRY-SPECIFIC DIRECTORIES

AdMedium Ivory Tower
uts.cc.utexas.edu/~admedium/ivorytower.html

All Search (2ask)
www.2ask.com/index_nomination.html

Beaucoup Search Engines
www.beaucoup.com

DirectoryGuide
www.directoryguide.com

FreeLinks: The Ultimate Web Site Traffic Builder
www.freelinks.com

I1INK: Free Link Sites
www.goodnet.com/~ej77486/linkmeu.htm

The Mining Co.–Web Search
websearch.miningco.com

InternetSales/Search Tools
www.Internet-sales.com/hot/search.shtml

Search.com
www.search.com

SelfPromotion.com
selfpromotion.com/sitelist

WebStep Top 100 Free Listings
www.mmgco.com/top100.html

REGIONAL DIRECTORIES

Link Exchange
directoryguide.linkexchange.com

Excite
www.excite.com/local/?action=browse

FAQ

FAQ (Frequently Asked Questions) sites are interesting in that they provide resources to their visitors on a variety of topics. You can request that the Webmaster include your book as a recommended resource.

RESOURCES FOR FINDING FAQ

BIZynet
www.bizynet.com/faq-news.htm

Internet FAQ Archives
www.faqs.org/faqs

54

MORE ESSENTIAL ONLINE RESOURCES

About.com's Publishing Page
publishing.about.com/business/publishing/mbody.htm
Wendy Butler covers everything from audio books to translation. Her site is an excellent resource with an extensive section on electronic publishing.

Amazon.com's Author Interviews
www.amazon.com/exec/obidos/recent-interviews/002-9055181-6288214
If you are a published author, fill out the online interview form!

Association of American Publishers
www.publishers.org/home/index.htm
The principal trade association of the book publishing industry.

Association of Canadian Publishers
www.publishers.ca
Represents over 135 Canadian-owned book publishers, with members from all provinces and members from the literary, general trade, education, and scholarly sectors.

BookFlash
www.bookflash.com
News about what's happening in the world of publishing, on and off the Internet. Subscribe to BookFlash bulletin at their Web site.

Bookwrights

www.bookwrights.com/nonfiction.html

They designed the cover of the original edition of this book, and they're outstanding!

Bookmarket

www.bookmarket.com

Book marketing, book promotion, and how to sell your books.

Bookzone

www.bookzone.com

New titles, publishing events, and announcements, Internet news—if it's about publishing, it's likely to show up here. News releases appear first [in the nreleases.html section] where they stay for thirty days. They are then archived [in areleases.html], where they'll be available indefinitely.

CheapPublicity.com

www.cheappublicity.com

Provides reporters, talk show hosts, and meeting organizers an easy and free way to locate authors, experts, and speakers.

dbusiness.com

www2.dbusiness.com/release

Post your press release for free.

Electronic Publishing: Fiction and Fact

www.asja.org/ewrongs.htm

E-wrongs about e-rights. Provided by the American Society of Journalists and Authors Contract Committee.

GuestFinder.com

www.guestfinder.com

Announce your availability as a media guest for a very reasonable cost.

Holt Uncensored

www.nciba.com/patholt.html

Pat Holt's candid look at books, authors, and the publishing industry is delivered via e-mail two times each week.

Focuses on independent bookselling.

Internet to Media Fax
www.imediafax.com
Customized news distribution service. Precisely target your media, choosing from thousands of print, TV, and radio media outlets.

InternetBookInfo
www.Internetbookinfo.com
The Internet Book Information Center, by W. Frederick Zimmerman.

IRIE Publishing and Productions
www.irie-publishing.com
Browse their site for multiple self-publishing hints and sign up for their free e-mag at *www.irie-publishing.com. /subscription.html.*

John Kremer's Book Marketing Tip of the Week
www.bookmarket.com/tips.html
Delivered weekly by e-mail.

Magazinedata
www.magazinedata.com/consumerdir.html
Phone, fax, and link directory for consumer magazines.

MediaFinder.com
www.mediafinder.com
Searchable database of more than 100,000 publications; also includes links to online media kits.

NewsletterAccess.com
www.newsletteraccess.com
Directory of over 5,000 print newsletters.

Newspaper Association of America
www.naa.org/hotlinks/index.asp
Large, searchable directory of Web sites for newspapers and other media.

Publisher's Marketing Association
www.pma-online.org/index.html
The largest nonprofit trade association representing independent publishers of books, audio, video, and CDs.

PRWeb
www.prweb.com/submit.htm
Post your press release for free.

Publist
www.publist.com
Searchable database of over 150,000 magazines, journals, newsletters, and other periodicals.

Raab Associates
www.raabassociates.com/tomarket.htm
Don't miss this one! Answers to questions on learning the ropes of PR, working with publishers, niche marketing, sales, self-publishing, editorial, tools of the trade, and more.

Scrub the Web
www.scrubtheweb.com
Not only is this site one of the newest search engines available, it will also help you peak and tweak your own Web site. After you enter your URL, it will check all of your site's META tags (the info that search engines grab to find your site) and then suggest to you ways of improving your odds of being listed in the major search engines. This service is free of charge and is sponsored by Advanced Business Systems of Arizona. The site also contains another free service that will automatically submit your URL to a large number of engines and directories.

Self Promotion.com
www.selfpromotion.com
Useful tools for sharpening your promotional quill. Helps you with the manual submission indexes such as Yahoo, though the process is geared as much to indexes as to search engines.

Smartbiz
www.smartbiz.com/sbs/arts/dun23.htm
Questions to ask when designing book promotions.

SPAN: Small Publishers Association of North America
www.spannet.org
Advances the image and profits of independent publishers through education and marketing opportunities.

Submit It!
www.submitit.com
One of the best submission services for your Web site.

The Tool Shed in the Cat's Backyard
hometown.aol.com/catspawpre/ToolShed.html
Super collection of prepublishing information.

The US All Media Jumpstation
www.owt.com/dircon/mediajum.htm-Mediajump
Direct Contact Publishing's comprehensive media guide to more than three thousand magazines, professional journals, trade and consumer publications.

The Woman's Guide to Self-Publishing Newsletter
www.irie-publishing.com/subscription.html
A networking and supportive environment for women in the publishing industry, particularly self-publishing.

Voice of the Shuttle
vos.ucsb.edu
Perhaps the most comprehensive and helpful directory to literary and general humanities materials on the Web, with a particular emphasis on academic research and writing.

WordWeaving.com
www.wordweaving.com
Brings together the reading and writing communities of the World Wide Web.

55

SUPPORT AND INTERACTIVE RESOURCES FOR AUTHORS

There are new lists being formed every day and we recommend you search the databases of these lists often. It's easy enough to sign up, read the posts for a few weeks, and decide if you want to participate.

For many of us, these listservs are the way we keep up with what is going on in the world of e-books and self-publishing.

1st Time Novelists Discussion List
www.egroups.com/community/1sttimenovelists
Converse with other beginning writers who are in the process of writing their first novel.

Author-L
www.egroups.com/community/Author-L
Author-L is a list for authors of both fiction and nonfiction books to discuss the business of writing. Topics of agents, editors, book proposals, publicity, productivity, writing conferences, book tours, Internet marketing, and more are open for discussion.

Authors
www.egroups.com/group/authors/info.html
Here is your chance to do a little networking with other writers. You will have the perfect opportunity to learn from established writers . . . find out how they got where they are today!

Authors Digest

www.egroups.com/community/AuthorsDigest.com

Share information with published and self-published authors as well as those writers who want to be.

Blackwriters-L

www.egroups.com/community/Blackwriters-L

A discussion list for anyone interested in writing, whether professionally or purely for self-expression. Offers black writers a forum for discussions on writing and writing-related topics; critiques and analyses of books, films, plays and poetry through the perspectives of writers (as opposed to readers); writing careers; educational options; the traditional and electronic publishing industries and more.

BookInAWeek

www.egroups.com/community/BookInAWeek

This mailing list is for any writer interested in taking part in regular Book-in-a-Week writing challenges. Official challenges are held every February and August in conjunction with the Romance Foretold writing Web site, but members of this list can organize mini-challenges amongst themselves.

Children's Writers and Illustrators

www.egroups.com/group/children-writers/info.html

This list is for discussion of writing (and illustrating) for children, including such topics as creativity, work styles and techniques, marketing and promotion, dealing with rejection, etc.

Christian_fic2

www.egroups.com/community/Christian_fic2

This listserv exists as a public forum for Christians who write genre literature, such as science fiction, fantasy, allegory, romance, Westerns, techno-thrillers, horror, mystery, and others following in the footsteps of other Christian writers such as C. S. Lewis, J. R. R. Tolkien, Dorothy L. Sayers, Charles Williams, Frank Peretti, and Stephen Lawhead. However, poets, nonfiction writers, and lurkers are very welcome here.

Creative Discussion

www.egroups.com/group/creative-discussion/info.html

A mailing list focusing on creative thought and the writing of poetry, stories, Web pages, and just about anything.

Creative Writers Critique Group

www.egroups.com/community/creativewriters

This list is dedicated to improving your writing skills, letting you meet and chat with other writers and just being able to exchange the creative flow.

Critic-Group—Critique Group

www.egroups.com/community/critic-group

This is a critique group for fantasy and science fiction writers. Submit your works and have the group give you suggestions: what is good, what is bad, and ways to fix it accordingly.

CWG

www.egroups.com/community/CWG

Christian Writers' Group. Discussion list for published or aspiring born-again writers. Purposes: to share ideas, tips, conference/seminar information, encouragement, support, and prayer requests. Editors and publishers also welcome.

DreamSong

www.egroups.com/community/dreamsong

DreamSong is for fantasy writers, a place to discuss their craft, bounce ideas back and forth, and generally just be there for one another, celebrating the successes and providing strength through the hard times.

E-guild

www.egroups.com/community/Eguild

E-guild is an organization of e-published authors (and those with a serious interest in e-publishing) with a number of purposes. Protecting authors' rights, educating the public about e-publishing, and promoting authors and their work are their primary concerns.

HumorWriting

www.egroups.com/community/HumorWriting

Do you want to learn how to write funny material? Would you like to meet other aspiring and published humor writers? Join and talk about the writing life, motivation, jokes, favorite comedians, and more! This list is moderated by Chandra K. Clarke, creator of the course "Humor Writing: The Art of Being Funny." She is also the author of the weekly column "In My Humble Opinion."

MUSE

www.egroups.com/community/M-U-S-E

This is a mailing list for young writers, mostly teens, who want to share their writing, talk about writing, reading, and so on, and get feedback or help others with their writing. MUSE is not censored.

PROSwrite

www.egroups.com/community/PROSwrite

Not for novices. This list is for *professional* writers, experienced contributors of nonfiction to print periodicals: for magazine staff, freelance, and those with editorial expertise. This is not a support group that teaches writing. Requirements: full understanding of the basics of writing and the marketing of writing.

ResearchForWriters

www.egroups.com/community/ResearchForWriters

This list is for anyone doing research for a book they are writing. List members can throw out a question and see if anyone knows the answer to it. Members also share interesting Web sites and books.

Rom-Critters

www.egroups.com/community/Rom-Critters

This is a critique forum for people who are actively and seriously pursuing a career in romance writing.

The Short Story Workshop

www.egroups.com/group/thessw/info.html

An online community of short fiction authors and poets. Featuring the following genres: comedy, fantasy, general, horror, mystery/crime, romance, and sci fi. Reviews, contests, chat, and much, much more.

StudyHall

www.egroups.com/community/StudyHall

Study Hall is a meeting place for writers of novel-length works who have finished a first draft and are actively seeking help in cleaning up their work to get it ready for publication or submission to an agent. It is primarily a critique group for all genres of novels. This is the perfect place for the serious writer who is looking for a place to help polish his/her work.

Women Who Write

www.egroups.com/community/womenwhowrite

This list is for women writers of all ages. Their literary efforts and aspirations can embrace various styles and mediums. Short stories, magazine articles, journals, poetry, prose, screenplays, TV scripts, etc. Women may be professional writers or amateurs.

Wordweave

www.egroups.com/community/Wordweave

Wordweave discussion list is part of the Wordweave Creative Writing Web site. The Wordweave list is like an open workshop at a writers' conference, a collaborative writing forum and inspirational resource center for the recreational and seasoned creative writer. Offers starter storylines (story seeds), collaborative fiction and nonfiction texts, and writing exercises for online and offline use. The Wordweave list offers information and tips as well as ongoing writing activities.

Writepro

www.egroups.com/community/writepro

Writepro is a subscription-only list made up only of members with more than three credits behind their name. It pertains to writing and writing problems.

My Writer Buddy

www.egroups.com/community/writerbuddy

My Writer Buddy is a free online correspondence club for writers of all ages, writing interests, and experience. Make new friends. Find a critique partner, mentor, or collaborator. Get moral support and encouragement from others who truly understand.

WriterTalk

www.egroups.com/community/WriterTalk

WriterTalk is a list where writers can gather and talk about their writing projects, their lives, their hopes and dreams. The WriterTalk list is a place where writers meet to socialize after a long, hard day of writing and marketing—as you might in a pub or coffeeshop.

The Write List

www.egroups.com/community/Write_List

The Write List is an e-mail group for writers of all levels of experience and all genres. Features include: writing tips, links to Web sites useful to writers, writing exercises, writing markets, submissions, critiques, and general discussion related to writing. Participation is encouraged but not required. The list is open to anyone regardless of their writing skills or experience.

YA Writer

www.egroups.com/community/YAWRITER

For those interested in writing young adult and middle grade books. This list is for discussion of craft, market, publishing, and other topics related to writing in these genres. Limited to fifty members. New subscribers will be put on a waiting list.

56

ONLINE DISCUSSION FORUMS

Ask Bill
www.insidetheweb.com/mbs.cgi/mb363954

***Inkspot*'s Writers' Forums**
www.writersbbs.com/bbs3

Mystery Place
www.talkcity.com/mystery

***Poets and Writers* Magazine Forum**
www.pw.org/speak.htm

WritersNet
www.writers.net/cgi-bin/WebX.cgi?writers

WritersNet for Agents and Editors
www.writers.net/cgi-bin/WebX.cgi?writers-14@3.KULnaoiLanP^0@.ee6ba05

WritersNet Publishing and Publishers
www.writers.net/cgi-bin/WebX.cgi?writers-14@3.KULnaoiLanP^0@.ee6b2b2

WritersNet Editing and Editors
www.writers.net/cgi-bin/WebX.cgi?writers-14@3.KULnaoiLanP^0@.ee6b2b0

WritersNet Writers and Writing
www.writers.net/cgi-bin/WebX.cgi?writers-14@3.KULnaoiLanP^0@.ee6b2ac

The Writers Quill Critique Center
www.insidetheweb.com/mbs.cgi/mb353149

57

E-MAGS FOR AUTHORS AND PUBLISHERS

All the Secrets

www.ozemedia.com

Free weekly e-mail newsletter for Internet entrepreneurs. Covers better business, computing, home office, marketing, mail-order, motivation, publicity, sales, telecommuting, and writing skills. This is one of Angela's favorites.

Children's Book Insider

www.write4kids.com

Tips, news, and advice for children's writers and illustrators—or those just dreaming of writing for kids.

The Coffeehouse Daily Grind

www.coffeehouseforwriters.com/courses.html

How do we successfully blend our writing into our daily chores and responsibilities? How do we pay bills, raise families, work day jobs (most of us have them, don't we?) and manage households without giving up writing time? Wonderful tips in this tip letter for writers.

ForeWord

www.forewordmagazine.com

ForeWord is a monthly news and review journal covering pertinent issues in the independent publishing industry.

Freebies for Writers

www.egroups.com/community/freebiesforwriters

Freebies for Writers is a free e-mail newsletter for writers of all genres. It's purpose is to connect writers with various forms of material for making life easier while they are waiting for their big break, as well as to help foster terrific ideas from free research materials.

Get Published!

www.getpub.com/archives.htm

This newsletter is for authors, e-zine editors, and independent publishers looking for help and advice on how to promote and publish their books and articles online. If you want to know how to self-publish your books or articles, want to know how to get published on the Internet, or need to know the steps to get published, then this newsletter is for you.

Internet Bookwatch

www.execpc.com/~mbr/bookwatch/ibw

A monthly book review magazine published by the *Midwest Book Review* and dedicated to reviews of fiction and nonfiction books of all kinds and categories. The average number of books reviewed per issue is approximately 450. Personal subscriptions via e-mail are free upon request. Individual reviews featured in the Internet Bookwatch can be posted to other thematically appropriate newsgroups, listservs, Web sites, and newsletters as long as the Internet Bookwatch is given credit.

The Internet Writing Journal

www.writerswrite.com/journal

Features articles on writing and getting published, interviews with editors, publishers, authors, and leaders in the media and the Internet, book and product reviews, as well as editorials and columns on current topics in the writing and publishing worlds and the Internet.

i-Tips

www.Internet-monitor.com

Published every other Monday, the i-Tips newsletter is written by marketing consultants specializing in the education and library markets. Topics cover market trends, marketing channels, Web site development, marketing on the Internet, and traditional marketing techniques such as direct mail, catalogs, advertising, and exhibits.

The Little Read Writers Hood

www.writershood.com

Monthly e-zine devoted to the writing of amateur authors.

PubLaw Update

www.publaw.com

Monthly newsletter containing information about copyright, trademarks, fair use, public domain, contracts, and other issues of interest to publishers and authors.

The Romantic Bower

www.theromanticbower.com

An online e-zine specializing in author promotions, publishing short fiction, reviews, poetry, and articles in all romance-related areas while maintaining a high quality of viewer-friendly material, support of romance novel book sales, and integration of romance-related material and information.

ShowIdeas.com

showideas.com/Join_Media_Mailing_List.htm

Where radio, TV, and print journalists turn for guest and show ideas. If you are an author or expert who wants publicity, you should be listed here. If you are a journalist seeking fresh guest and show ideas, you should visit this site often.

Whispers of Love

www.addicted-to-romance.com

Each issue contains a feature article about love or romance, top five romantic tips of the month, a profile of a romantic musician and sample music, a how-to article for people interested in writing romance, and a romance poll. Select issues will also feature additional articles, short stories, romance book excerpts, or other news pertaining to love, romance, dating, and relationships in general.

Write to Publish

www.author.co.uk/ezine-subscribe.htm

An updated guide to the *author.co.uk,* with hints and suggestions for writers, news of new books on the site, and details of events that may interest writers, especially those who publish their own work.

The Writing Child
www.klockepresents.com
Biweekly newsletter for young writers to help promote self-esteem in children. Parents are welcome to subscribe and contribute.

The Writing Parent
www.klockepresents.com
Newsletter for parents, grandparents, and others to help you reach your writing goals without blaming the kids.

AUTHORS' AND SMALL PUBLISHERS' FAQ

Where can I get an ISBN?
www.bowker.com/standards/home/isbn

Where can I obtain copyright forms?
lcweb.loc.gov/copyright

What cannot be copyrighted?
www.smartbiz.com/sbs/arts/hrc3.htm

Where can I find copyright laws organized by country?
www.self-publishing.com/copyright-links.html

What is a trademark?
www.law.cornell.edu/topics/trademark.html

When is it opinion and when is it libel?
www.novalearn.com/wol/archives/kaa8.htm

Where can I learn more about publishing law?
www.publaw.com

Where can I do a quick dictionary/thesaurus search?
www.self-publishing.com/references.html

Where can I download a sample e-book to use for formatting?
www.booklocker.com/sampleebook.zip

How do I buy illustrations or cover art?
www.writersweekly.com/bookediting.htm

What's an EAN and a UPC?
www.abiogenesis.com/AbioDocs/ISBN.html

How do I use a pen name?
www.scalar.com/mw/pages/faw1.html

How do I determine the price of my book?
www.suite101.com/article.cfm/self-publishing/13118
www.smartbiz.com/sbs/columns/dbook7.htm

How do I spot literary scams?
www.novalearn.com/wol.Strauss11a.htm

What does the National Writers Union say about e-book contracts?
www.nwu.org//docs/online%2Dp.htm

How do I sell foreign rights to my book?
www.smartbiz.com/sbs/columns/dbook31.htm

Where can I find an agent?
www.publishersweekly.com/AAR
nt9.nyic.com/literaryagent/sch-page.html
www.writers.net/agents.html

What questions should I ask a potential agent?
www.inkspot.com/market/agentlist.html

What can I expect from an agent?
www.novalearn.com/wol/archives/kress11-2.htm

Where are some smaller online bookstores where I can sell my book?

BooksAMillion.com
www.booksamillion.com
In order to be listed here, your book must be made available through American Wholesale Book Company, Ingram, or Baker & Taylor.

Chapters
www.chapters.ca
You need to call them at the phone number on their Web site to request to be added.

Indigo
www.indigo.ca
Like Borders, Indigo automatically add books once they're listed in Books in Print.

Powells
www.powells.com

Where can I learn more about marketing to libraries?
www.combinedbook.com/myths.html
www.mont.lib.md.us/marketing.html

Where can I sell autographed books online?
www.autographedbyauthor.com

Where can I find the online bestseller lists?

American Booksellers Association
www.bookweb.org/booksense/bestsellers

Amazon.com
www.amazon.com/exec/obidos/subst/lists/best/bestsellers.html

Barnes & Noble
www.bn.com/bestsellers/index.asp

The Boston Globe
ae.boston.com/arts/books/bestsellers/pfiction.html
ae.boston.com/arts/books/bestsellers/nonfiction.html

Evangelical Christian Publishers Association
ecpa.org/ECPA/bestsellers.html

Independent Booksellers
www.notachain.com

The New York Times
www.nytimes.com/books/yr/mo/day/bsp

Publishers Weekly
www.publishersweekly.com/bestsellersindex.asp

USA Today
www.usatoday.com/life/enter/books/leb1.htm

Where can I find a list of TV and radio broadcasters?
archive.comlab.ox.ac.uk/publishers/broadcast

Where can I find more book review resources?
authors.miningco.com/arts/authors/msub21rev.htm

What can I do about a bad book review?
www.writersweekly.com/angelafeatures.htm#bbr

Where can I find a directory of writers, editors, publishers, and agents?
www.writers.net

Where can I find a directory of writers' organizations?
www.inkspot.com/tk/network/assoc.htm

Where can I network with professional self-published authors?
Send any e-mail to *publish-subscribe@onelist.com*

Where can I find a free directory of self-published authors?
www.published.com

Where can I find some personal experiences of self-published authors?
www.self-publishing.com/inthetrenches.html

What are some self-publishing mistakes I can avoid?
www.about%2dbooks.com/article6.htm

Where can I find a directory of critique groups?
www.inkspot.com/craft/critique.html

What is a really good resource for publishing information online?
www.hkbu.edu.hk/~ppp/WASP.html

Where can I find a list of book fairs and events?
www.spannet.org
Click on "publishing events."

Where can I post excerpts of my novel?
bitbooks.com/about.htm

Where can I promote my Web site for free?

FreeLinks
www.freelinks.com
Find all the tools and resources necessary to promote your Web site.

VirtualPromote
www.virtualpromote.com
Excellent resource! Learn to promote your Web site and 1,000 places to do it.

WebStep
www.mmgco.com/top100.html
Online, hyperlinked, annotated index of the best search engines, databases, and yellow pages that will allow you to register for free.

Go-Net Wide
www.gonetwide.com/gopublic.html
Direct links to Web site URL submission forms for essential Internet resources.

Where can I announce my new Web site?

Netscape's What's New
www.netscape.com/escapes/submit_new.html

New Page List
web-star.com/newpage/newpage.html

NCSA What's New
www.ncsa.uiuc.edu/SDG/Software/Mosaic/Docs/whats-new-form.html

What's New Too!
nu2.com

Where can I submit my Web site to multiple search engines for free?

Add It!
www.123add-it.com
Submit your site to over thirty different places on the Web all at one time for free. Check out the Online Web Promotion Manual.

Add Me!
www.addme.com
This free service allows you to submit your Web site to the thirty most popular search engines and directories on the Web. Be sure to sign up for their free e-mag!

AutoSubmit
autosubmit.com/promote.html
Enter your site information once, and then submit it to the biggest search engines on the Net.

Submit It!
www.submit-it.com/sitrial.htm
Makes it easy to submit your URLs to a variety of online catalogs so people from around the world will be able to find your page.

Where can I find a list of publishing associations?
publishing.about.com/business/publishing/msub1.htm

Where can I find current book publishing news?
www.moreover.com/bookpublishing

Where can I find resources on banned books and censorship?
www.inkspot.com/other/banned.html

What should I put in my press kit?
www.raabassociates.com/topic1.htm

How do I prepare for a television interview?
www.raabassociates.com/topic1.htm

How do book clubs work?
www.spl.lib.wa.us/wacentbook/bookclub.html

What are some online book clubs I can pitch my book to?

A&E Bookclub
www.aande.com/bookclub

AdBooks
www.geocities.com/SoHo/Village/3503
Discusses books for young adults.

Book Chatter
www.bookchatter.tierranet.com

The Book Group List
books.rpmdp.com

Book Lovers
www.mindmills.net/booklovers

The Booksies
www.geocities.com/Athens/Aegean/2515

Book Woman Book Discussion Group
www.womensites.com/bookwoman/bdg_list.htm
Every three months, they nominate books they would like to discuss as a group.

BookWorms Virtual Book Club
www.geocities.com/Athens/Styx/3544

The Coffee Will Make You Black Reading Group
www.aalbc.com/discussion/Instructions.htm

Constant Reader
www.constantreader.com

MysteryNet
discuss.mysterynet.com

The Online Reading Group
userpage.fu-berlin.de/~tanguay/readclub.htm
Members submit book reviews.

The Rogue Book Club
members.tripod.com/~bookgroup

Science Fiction Reading Club
www.geocities.com/Area51/7118

Senior.net Book and Literature Discussion Forum
www.seniornet.org

Utne Readers Book Club
cafe.utne.com/cafe
Requires free registration.

Wired for Books
www.tcom.ohiou.edu/books

Women.com
women.com/clubs/book.html

What are the best book-related Usenet newsgroups?
rec.arts.books.reviews
rec.arts.books.childrens
rec.arts.books

rec.arts.sf.written
rec.arts.mystery
rec.arts.poems
rec.arts.books.marketplace
rec.arts.prose
rec.arts.books.reviews (moderated)
rec.arts.sf.reviews
misc.books.technical
rec.arts.int-fiction
alt.books.technical
alt.books.mysteries
alt.books.reviews
clari.living.books   news about books and authors (moderated)
fj.rec.food   food, cooking, cookbooks, and recipes
misc.books.technical   discussion of books about technical topics
relcom.fido.su.books   fidonet, for book readers and lovers

What are the best publishing-related Usenet newsgroups?

alt.union.natl-writers   publishing industry & labor movement
alt.publish.books   for independent book publishers
bit.listserv.vpiej-l   electronic publishing
comp.publish.electronic.misc   general electronic publishing issues
ieee.pub.general   publishing activities, general discussion
rec.arts.books   books of all genres, and the publishing industry
ieee.pub.announce   publishing activities, announcements
thelinq.ebooks   all about electronic books (moderated)

What are the best Usenet newsgroups for authors?

alt.prose.memoir   a forum for journalistic authors
clari.living.books   news about books and authors
alt.books.purefiction   discussion of bestselling novels and how to write them

Where can I read more about successful e-serial authors?

Stephen King
wired.com/news/culture/0,1284,37867,00.html

Seth Godin
wired.com/news/culture/0,1284,37600,00.html

Douglas Clegg
www.wired.com/news/culture/0,1284,34499,00.html

What is the highest-paying e-book award?
wired.com/news/culture/0,1284,37599,00.html

Where can I list and market my own e-serial?
www.inboxfiction.com

M. J. Rose

Like it or not, people say no more than they say yes. But when I started out on my own in the publishing business I got paralyzed by the first few dozen no's that I heard. Rejection is tough on even the most self-confident person. Like a hammer, each no sank me lower into a funk. My idea was good, wasn't it? But would so many people say no if it had potential?

What made it even worse was that I'm a writer and my business idea was based on my own writing, so every no sounded even louder and had far-reaching repercussions. Was the writing itself bad or just the business idea bad? And if the writing wasn't good and if I couldn't get this idea off the ground, I'd have to give up writing full-time and take a nine-to-five job back in the corporate world. *Oh no!*

I began having dreams where every participant spoke a stilted version of the English language. No matter what the question, the answer was no. I imagined a character in a children's book named Princess No-No. I saw the letters n-o inside of other words like soprano, piano, and stenographer.

Sometimes I would whisper "yes" out loud to myself just to make sure the word still existed.

I was telling a friend, who is a professional fundraiser, about my dilemma. She laughed and told me that in her business the no's are a good thing. "For each no you are getting closer to a yes," she said. She even had a mathematical equation she'd worked out from ten years of experience. She had to get fifteen no's to get a yes. And since she was asking for contributions for a worthwhile charity, her no-to-yes ratio would be lower than mine would. I could count on a thirty-to-one no-to-yes ratio.

So I started to tally the no's.

In the first two weeks I got ten no's.

In the second two weeks, twelve no's. (I was starting to get excited, twenty-two no's down, only eight to go. Finally after six weeks and thirty-four no's, I heard one wonderful, resonant, *yes*. (These no's and yes's were about getting a major reviewer to agree to read my self-published novel.)

A funny thing happened to me in those weeks. I went from dreading and hating the no's to understanding something about them. They represented hard work and determination on my part. I was proud of those no's. Plus, the no's were important. They weeded out the people I really didn't want to review the novel anyway. Only someone who truly was open to the idea that a self-published novel could be any good was the right person to read it.

So if you are searching for reviewers, participation in a project, looking for a partner or for financing, expect to hear a lot of no's. Will you ever become immune to them? Well, no.

But can you get to a point where you can deal with them?

Yes, you betcha!

Angela Adair-Hoy

I've heard stories about authors taking long, exotic vacations after completing a book. Believe me, after the past months of researching, writing, and scratching my head into the wee hours of the morning, every single day of the week, I sure could use one! And I certainly understand how an author can feel entitled to such a break between books.

But, how do those authors make a profit by lounging on a yacht between novels? Perhaps the bestselling authors can afford to do that, knowing their books will sell on their names alone. That won't work for me, however!

Starting tomorrow, I'm not taking a year off, or even a day. I'm going to join M. J. in the publicity campaign she launched even before we started writing this book. Within only a few days of deciding the title, she had already generated press for this book. By the following week, she had generated a whole lot more. Now, we have both appeared in dozens of print and online publications, all of which mention or link to the Web page for this book: *www.publishandpromote.com.*

It seems like every day since we've started this, M. J. has called with such surprises as, "Hey, you're gonna be quoted in *Time* magazine next week" and "*The New York Times* called this morning" and "Did that woman call you about that interview this morning?" and "Angie, run down to Barnes & Noble to pick up *Business 2.0,* and turn to page 266" and "I'm sorry I didn't call earlier. I was doing a radio interview" and "Did you tell that woman that you *can* speak in Manhattan in January?" and, jeez, I could go on and on and on.

Know how she does it? She uses all the secrets listed in this book . . . and the press comes calling, several times a week. E-mails, phone calls, interviews, speaking requests, and more. And, every bit of press sells copies of this book.

Yes, you can follow in our footsteps, and yes, you can use our secrets and everyone else's here to pave your own self-publishing success story. If you do, we'd love to profile you in the next edition of this book. The Internet is an ever-changing medium and we will never lack for new content and new online publicity campaign strategies!

So, what are you waiting for? Start your book publicity campaign today, right here, right now. We'll be waiting to hear about your book's success, and we'll want to know what secrets you've picked up along the way!

From both of us: To all the wonderful contributors who gave so generously of their time and wisdom to make this book possible. Without them, we'd all make lots of mistakes trying to follow in their footsteps.

To our agent, Loretta Barrett, who makes it all happen.

To our editor, Hope Dellon at St. Martin's Press, for seeing this book's potential and being a delight to work with, as well as to her assistant editor, Maureen Drum, for her painstaking attention to detail to make us look perfect on paper.

From M. J. Rose: To Doug Scofield for his insight, inspiration, and stead-fast belief that this book should be written.

To Angela's husband and children for not complaining (too much) about the time she spent at her computer getting this book done.

To Jeff Bezos and Diane Zoi for truly leveling the playing field and creating an opportunity for authors to forge ahead on their own.

Last but certainly not least, thanks go to Dr. Marc Lorber and the Yale/New Haven Transplant Unit. In their honor a portion of my proceeds of this book will be going to the National Kidney Foundation.

From Angela Adair-Hoy: To my children, Zach, Ali, and Frank, for their understanding and for forcing me to take breaks when my eyes were crossed. And my husband, Richard, for patting my shoulder, reading over my shoulder, and not uttering one complaint about that massive pile of neglected laundry.

To M. J.'s new puppy for her calming influence and Doug for standing by patiently when M. J. talked to me on the phone for hours . . . and hours.

To John D. Barringer, author of *Daddy's Girl: Women Dealing with Father Issues* (http://www.booklocker.com/authors/ibarringer.html), for never, ever letting me stop believing in myself and my dreams.

Advance: The amount paid to an author in anticipation of royalties to be earned upon publication.

ARCs (Advance Reading Copies or Advance Review Copies): Copies of a book or galleys sent out for review prior to the publication date.

ASCII (American Standard Code for Information Interchange): A set of numerical codes used by computers to represent text and basic punctuation. Computers use ASCII to encode text (such as found in an e-mail message) when transferring it from one computer to another.

Attachment: A text, graphic, or program file that is transmitted along with an e-mail message.

Backlist: Books previously published yet still in print.

Banner: An advertisement—either graphic or text—appearing on a Web page or in an e-mail message.

BBS (Bulletin Board System): An electronic message center catering to a specific group of people with a common interest.

Blurb: A very short sentence or phrase used to sell/market a product or service.

Book Packager: A person or company that puts book deals together. Can also refer to a firm that edits, designs, and/or prints books for publishers that do not have this capability in-house.

Browser: Short for Web browser—software used to locate and display Web pages.

CD-ROM (Compact Disc Read-Only Memory): A disk, read by a

CD-ROM drive, universal in size and capable of storing up to 650 megabytes of graphics, sound, and video data.

CD-R Drive (Compact Disk-Recordable drive): Also called a CD burner, this is a disk drive used to create CD-ROMs and audio CDs.

Cookie: A text code passed between a Web browser and a Web server that is used to help identify users. They can reference or encode personal information only if the user first gives that information to the Web site.

Copyediting: Editing a manuscript for errors in content, grammar, and spelling.

Copyright: The ownership of intellectual property defined by law.

Cyber-: A prefix used in new terms created to describe various kinds of computer communications.

Cyberspace: The virtual world of connected computer systems.

Discussion List: A list of participants discussing via e-mail a topic of common interest. Also known as a listserv.

Download: To copy a computer file from its main source to another computer.

Domain Name: A name used in a URL to identify Web pages.

E-Book (electronic book): A book delivered in electronic format, as an electronic document, which must be accessed using a computer or hand-held reading device. Some e-books are delivered as electronic downloads to a buyer's computer and some are sent via electronic mail (e-mail), while others are sent via regular mail on a CD-ROM or computer disk to the buyer.

E-Commerce (electronic commerce): Conducting business online and/or transferring funds electronically.

Electronic Rights: Copyrights to an electronic document.

E-Mag (electronic magazine): An electronic publication delivered by e-mail to paying or nonpaying subscribers.

E-Mail (electronic mail): The very rapid transmission of messages and data over communications networks.

E-Publishing (electronic publishing): To publish in electronic format.

E-Publisher (electronic publisher): Publishing firm that publishes books in electronic format.

Encryption: The conversion of data into a format that cannot be read without the proper authorization or software.

Excel: A spreadsheet software program manufactured by Microsoft.

E-Zine (electronic zine): An electronic publication delivered by e-mail or published on a Web page.

FAQ (Frequently Asked Questions): A document or Web page that lists questions and answers about a specific topic.

Footer: The phrase appearing repeatedly at the bottom of every page of a document.

FTP (File Transfer Protocol): A standard procedure used on the Internet for transmitting files.

Galleys: The preliminary typeset version of manuscript; the term is sometimes used interchangeably with ARCs.

Genre: The literary category of a novel, such as romance, science fiction, mystery, and so on.

GIF (Graphic Interchange Format): graphic file format.

Graphics: Objects (pictures) that can be displayed using a specific type of hardware or software.

Hit: Every time Web browser software retrieves the files necessary to build a Web page from a Web site. If a Web page is comprised of some text and two graphics, this would total three hits—one for the actual Web page and one for each graphic.

Home Page (or Homepage): A Web site's main, or opening, Web page.

Host: The primary computer where a Web site or computer file resides.

HTML (Hypertext Markup Language): A set of tags that tells Web browser software how it should display the content of a Web page. Example: the HTML code: <B>text</B> tells a Web browser to display the word "text" in boldface.

HTTP (Hypertext Transfer Protocol): The protocol used to define how information should be transmitted between Web servers and Web browsers.

Imprint: A specific line of books offered by a publisher.

Internet: The network connecting millions of computers around the globe.

IP Address (Internet Protocol Address): A unique series of numbers used to identify a computer or device on the Internet.

IRC (Internet Relay Chat): A specific online chat system (created by Jarkko Oikarinen of Finland) that caters to multiple chat participants.

ISBN (International Standard Business Number): A ten-digit number, unique to each book and each edition of a book, used by publishers, libraries, and booksellers to identify books.

ISP (Internet Service Provider): A firm that connects a company or individual to the Internet.

JPEG (Joint Photographic Experts Group): A compression technique for color graphics.

Link: A connection between Web pages, or between a Web page and a file, that takes a user instantly to that other Web page or file when he or she clicks on it. Also known as a hot link.

LISTSERV®: An automatic mailing list server created by Eric Thomas.

LISTSERVER/LISTSERV: A computer that hosts and manages mailing lists.

LOGIN: The procedure to access a computer system, usually requiring a username and password.

Macintosh (Mac): A computer model created by Apple Computer, which uses a different operating software platform and applications than a PC (personal computer).

Mass Market Paperback: A paperback book that is usually smaller in format and less expensive, and has a wider sales distribution, than traditional trade paperbacks.

Message Board: A Web page where messages are posted by people with a common interest, often linked according to message and response.

Midlist: Books that show promise but that are not expected to be big sellers.

Modem (modulator–demodulator): A device used to transmit data from a computer to a telephone line.

MS (plural MSS): Manuscript.

MSWord (Microsoft Word): A popular and widely-used word processing program developed by Microsoft and used on PCs.

Netiquette: Internet etiquette used when posting electronic messages.

Network: A group of computers linked together.

Newsgroup: A type of online discussion group contained within the USENET.

Online: Connected to a computer service through a modem.

Opt-in: To agree voluntarily to receive specific types of electronic messages from a list or Web site or on a specific topic.

PC (Personal Computer): Type of computer that usually runs on Microsoft Windows applications.

PDF (Portable Document Format): A file format created by Adobe Systems that enables a file to be transmitted and received in its original format. The author of the file can also set the security options at a high level, preventing readers from manipulating the document in any way.

Periodical: A publication issued at regular intervals (weekly, monthly, annually, etc.).

Plagiarism: The theft of intellectual property by falsely representing oneself as the author of another's work.

POD (Print-on-Demand): The process of printing books quickly and economically, one at a time, from stored electronic files, instead of printing large quantities all at once.

Post: To publish a message online.

Proofreading: Checking a manuscript or book for typographical errors.

Remainders: Books that did not sell out their print run and are offered at a very high discount.

Returns: Books that were initially ordered by booksellers but were returned to the publisher because they did not sell to consumers.

Royalties: A percentage of the price of each book sold that is paid to the author.

Search Engine: A Web site that lets users enter key words to search for documents and Web pages.

Self-publish: To publish one's own works, including paying all publication costs and retaining all sales income.

Server: A computer connected to the Internet (or a private computer network) that allows other computers to connect to it to retrieve files and/or execute programs.

Slush Pile: The stack of unsolicited manuscripts sitting in a publisher's office waiting for consideration.

SMTP (Simple Mail Transfer Protocol): A protocol used for sending e-mail messages.

Spam: Unsolicited electronic junk mail.

Subsidiary Rights: Rights sold by the publisher or agent to other publishing outlets (book club rights, foreign language rights, etc.).

Subsidy Publisher: A publisher that charges the author for the cost of publishing their book; also called a Vanity Publisher.

Trade Paperback: A book with a similar size and appearance as its hardcover counterpart, but bound with a quality paper cover.

URL (Uniform Resource Locator): The address of a resource (Web site, document, program) on the Internet.

Usenet: The network that makes newsgroups and information accessible from the Internet.

USP (Unique Selling Proposition): A one-line description that defines the unique appeal of an item being offered for sale.

Vanity Publisher: *See* Subsidiary Publisher.

Virtual: Generated by computer, without physical form and substance.

Web: The abbreviation for the World Wide Web (see WWW).

Web Site: The location on the WWW of a home page and its subpages.

WWW (World Wide Web): The network of Internet servers using the HTTP protocol.

INDEX

M. J. Rose (*www.mjrose.com*) Rose's erotic suspense novel, *Lip Service,* gained a flurry of media attention when it became the first self-published novel and the first e-book to be discovered on the Web (at Amazon.com to be exact) by the New York publishing giants.

Lip Service is also the first self-published novel and e-book chosen by the Doubleday Book Club and the Literary Guild as a Featured Alternate Selection. Just months after being self-published and becoming Amazon.com's highest ranked small-press novel, *Lip Service* was picked up by Pocket Books and published as a hardcover in September of 1999; it was subsequently published in Germany, the Netherlands, Australia, France, and England.

Rose's other novels include *Private Places,* a novella only available at *www.mightywords.com,* and *In Fidelity,* published in 2001 by Pocket Books. Rose has appeared on *The Today Show, Pure Oxygen,* in *Time* magazine, *Working Woman* magazine, *The New York Times, Publishers Weekly, The LA Times, The Washington Post, Business 2.0, Forbes, Wired News, Salon.com,* and *Poets and Writers* magazine. Rose also writes columns and articles about the book business for several e-zines and magazines including *Wired News,* and she is on the advisory board of *Writer's Digest* magazine.

Before becoming a full-time author, she was the creative director of a New York ad agency, Rosenfeld, Sirowitz and Lawson. It is her unique combination of marketing know-how and advertising knowledge that helped her self-promote her own novels. Write to her at: *MJRoseAuthor@ aol.com.*

Angela Adair-Hoy (*www.writersweekly.com*) Adair-Hoy is one of the most prolific and profitable self-published authors in the Internet today. Sales of her e-books alone exceed $5,000 every month. Her marketing savvy has helped other authors obtain literary recognition and financial independence. The gross monthly revenues generated from her two Web sites are astounding, considering that the companies are run from a small desk in the corner of her bedroom.

Angela Adair-Hoy was a television reporter in Woodlands, Texas, prior to joining the publishing industry as president of Deep South Syndicate. She and her husband own Booklocker (*www.booklocker.com*), the most author-friendly e-book publisher on the Internet, paying generous royalties of up to 70 percent.

She also publishes *WritersWeekly,* one of the highest-traffic writing Web sites in the world, as well as *The Write Markets Report,* a monthly electronic magazine (e-mag) featuring new and updated markets for freelance writers and journalists. Adair-Hoy has and continues to author and publish a variety of how-to books for freelance writers and authors, all of which focus on helping writers make a living doing what they love. *WritersWeekly* offers a free, weekly e-mag featuring new freelance job listings and paying markets. New subscribers receive a free e-book, *How to Be a Freelance Writer: Includes 103 Paying Markets.* Subscription information is at the Web site.

Adair Hoy resides in Maine with her husband, well-known Internet marketing expert Richard Hoy, and their three children, Zach, Ali, and Frank. Her daughter, Ali, became a published (and paid) writer at the age of six and is now the editor in chief of Booklocker Jr.

ONLINE UPDATES!

Web site addresses and e-mails can change overnight. We provide updates to the links appearing in this book at: *www.publishandpromote.com.*

WHERE TO SEND YOUR SECRETS, SUCCESSES, AND SUGGESTIONS!

If you have a secret, a success story, or an online resource that our readers must know about, please send it by e-mail to *angela@publishandpromote. com.*